Jacky Hyams

Time to Help Your Parents

A practical guide to recognising problems and providing support

piatkus

PIATKUS

First published in Great Britain in 2007 by Piatkus Books Ltd
This paperback edition published in 2010 by Piatkus

A CIP catalogue record for this book
is available from the British Library.

ISBN 978-0-7499-4065-2

Text design by Briony Hartley
Edited by Anthea Matthison

Typeset by Phoenix Photosetting, Chatham, Kent
Printed and bound in Great Britain by
CPI Mackays, Chatham ME5 8TD

Papers used by Piatkus are natural, renewable and recyclable
products sourced from well-managed forests and certified
in accordance with the rules of the Forest Stewardship Council.

Mixed Sources
Product group from well-managed
forests and other controlled sources
www.fsc.org Cert no. SGS-COC-004081
© 1996 Forest Stewardship Council

FSC

Piatkus
An imprint of
Little, Brown Book Group
100 Victoria Embankment
London EC4Y 0DY

An Hachette UK Company
www.hachette.co.uk

www.piatkus.co.uk

Contents

Acknowledgements

This book could not have been written without the assistance and co-operation of a number of people who willingly donated their time to help me. My most sincere thanks go to: Clare Wheeler at Camden Carers; Leon Smith at Nightingale; Deborah Clatworthy and Clarissa Murdoch at The Whittington Hospital NHS Trust; Catherine Collins, RD, St George's Hospital NHS Trust; Stephen Burke and Caroline Bernard, Counsel and Care; Imelda Redmond, Carers UK; Mervyn Kohler, Help the Aged; Mary MacLeod, Family and Parenting Institute; Diana Whitworth, Grandparents Plus; Owain Wright, Saga Personal Finance; Liz Urben, Red Cross; Anjoula Sharman, Cruse Bereavement Service; Ann Richardson, BeingAnOnly. Special thanks for their valuable insights also go to Christopher Manthorp, Denise Knowles and Julia Cole.

And finally, all thanks and gratitude to my mother, Molly Margaret Hyams, an inspirational parent if ever there was one.

Introduction

This book is dedicated to our parents. Yet in a sense, it's about all of us too. Because, although the book is aimed at families who might be concerned about what will happen to their parents as they grow older and need more help, the reality is, of course, we're all getting older. And times are changing. By 2030 over half of the UK's population will be over 50. Life expectancy is rising. And the year 2007 was an important anniversary: for the first time in our history, pensioners outnumbered children in the UK. So it's in everyone's interest to know more about growing old.

Yet until recently, our attitudes to ageing have been far from enlightened. It's not exactly a topic that most of us focus on in the frantic rush of modern life. When I started researching this book, I repeatedly found myself being told by age care or health professionals that most families meet or contact them in a state of total shock – completely unprepared for the reality that parents may have grown perilously frail or can't manage at home any more.

Why this ignorance? I put it down to human nature: a tendency to distance or separate ourselves from the starker truths. It is, after all, much easier to focus on the here and now and push the difficult or unappealing thoughts about old age, sickness and mortality to one side. And who can blame us? In the main, our society is in thrall to youth.

Yet, in another way, maybe the prevailing emphasis on youth and energy has served a good purpose, since many of today's seventy- and eightysomethings are awesomely independent and youthful in their attitude: as people live longer and once life-threatening conditions become treatable, they're no longer prepared to fade into the background or behave like previous older generations. It is more than likely that your parents are currently leading independent, active lives, travelling often, living abroad, experiencing lifestyles their own parents would have found unimaginable. That sweet, bespectacled, sock-knitting, white-haired granny of yore may still exist, but she's not always readily recognisable nowadays.

Blame entrenched social attitudes to youth worship if you will, but I'm no different to most people. Until recent years, I remained pretty ignorant about matters relating to growing older. Old was another country and a distant one at that. I certainly hadn't spent much time around my elders. My maternal grandparents died not long after I was born. My father's parents were around until my early teens and, as a toddler, I saw them regularly. But their impact on my life was distant, even fleeting.

I lived abroad for many years and my father died while I lived in Australia. Even my work as a journalist rarely brought me into contact with the realities of later life like care homes or age-related illnesses (that says something about many editors' attitudes to enlightening readers, but that's another story). It was only some years after I'd returned to live in the UK, when my mother, Molly, then 82, fell over and broke her hip – a typical scenario for many families with older parents living independently – that my own journey began into learning about the myriad issues that emerge when a parent needs your help.

And there can be many issues involved: NHS hospitals, social workers, local authorities, primary care trusts, care workers, sheltered housing, residential care, let alone age-related complaints or illnesses. How many of us, other than those whose work brings them into contact with these areas, know much about how such organisations work – and, most importantly, how they can help us support our parents?

I had one big advantage: I could juggle my working hours as a freelance and had time to visit my mother frequently, track down information, hassle local-authority staff, liaise with social services, hire independent help and eventually inspect care homes.

I live alone, I'm self-employed and I don't have children. So the demands on my time are less than they are for many others. But through it all, I wondered: how did people like me, wanting to do everything possible, help one – or even both – parents cope with all this emotionally, as well as practically when, almost overnight, your parent becomes almost a child? You love your parents. But how do you – and they – cope with a sudden role reversal? And if so much of your time is already taken up by partners, adult children and grandchildren, let alone busy jobs or careers, how can you maintain some sort of balance, rushing from hospital or care home to work and back, trying to do your best, hoping against hope that your efforts are not in vain?

I have tried to answer these difficult questions in this book. In my own case, as I struggled to handle the increasingly complicated logistics of helping Molly, living alone in sheltered housing but gradually losing the ability to fend for herself, I discovered that the general ignorance about the topic of helping ageing parents extended even to people who had already lived through this difficult time.

I talked to friends, many of whom had already been through similar experiences. Some had lost their parents. Yet their stories, while often poignant, were of scant help to me in a practical sense. Why? Because each person's story is a little bit different; each relationship with loved ones has its own nuance or subtlety. And while this book endorses the value of sharing your concerns with relatives or close friends, it was all too apparent, when I poured out my frustrations, that discussing your feelings will help – but only up to a point. You still need to be hugely resourceful when it comes to going out and finding help on a day-to-day level. And the emotions involved in looking out for a parent with failing independence can sometimes overwhelm you and hinder your progress. So you do need to understand more about your own reactions to what's happening.

This book has been born out of a strong desire to pass on what I did learn and give you the information to help enhance your parents' later years, whatever your circumstances. (You might, of course, be looking to help an aunt, a cousin or even a grandparent or friend, but for simplicity's sake I've used the term 'parents' as a catch-all description.)

So many different topics are involved, I have had to abbreviate some of the information out of sheer necessity.

Certain medical topics, for instance, merit an entire book to themselves. The same goes for the two million plus people in the UK who care for elderly relatives in their home on a full-time basis. They deserve every bit of recognition and respect society can muster. But from the outset, I've been aware that not everyone who reads this book will find themselves in this situation. So I have also had to abbreviate the section regarding full-time caring, but I have included pointers to valuable sources of advice. The information you might need is out there – it's just a case of knowing where to go for it.

What you will find in this book are ideas for tackling key topics, such as diet, hospital, family relationships, sourcing help/care and, of course, the dilemma of moving. Most people want to remain in their own home in later years, no matter how frail they might become. It's a right that very few would dare to challenge. And it's certainly foremost in government thinking as it looks ahead to the changing needs of an increasingly older population.

After spending many years visiting my mother in residential care, one thing stands out: when residential care works properly and focuses squarely on every aspect of helping older people live dignified, happy lives, despite frailties, then there are good ideas there to be taken away and used in the home.

Those ideas are often everyday things but they can make a significant difference to an elderly relative's life – provided someone cares enough to think of them. Of course everyone should have a clean, secure, safe environment to live in and good healthcare available as they grow older. But frequently, it is the 'smaller' things like laughter, music, communication, shared memory and a sense of belonging that enrich people's lives, wherever they live, no matter how restricted they might be physically or mentally. All that's required is a bit of thought and input from family or friends into making these ordinary pleasures happen. So this book also includes many of those suggestions: tips that might help your parents get that much more out of life.

The major decisions, of course, like deciding to move, can't be set down in black and white terms. Most people fear change. We worry about the responsibility of steering our parents in the wrong direction. This book isn't about telling them to do anything – it's about trying to help them reach a comfortable frame of mind, whatever their choices. As for decision making, I have placed due emphasis on the need for good communication between parents and children. At any age, if people don't express their needs or feelings to each other, what's left unsaid can leave a dangerous void.

Of course, in later life, that willingness to share feelings becomes even more important. Yes, every family is different in the way it behaves and the way its members interact with each other. And people do sometimes face incredible resistance when they endeavour to steer parents into getting more help: it's a fact of life. But the families I talked to in my research whose parents are happy with the big decisions they've made all said the same thing: 'We discussed it with Mum and Dad and they said they wanted to do this.'

Throughout my research I've also been conscious of the varying circumstances families face. Different lives need different approaches. Many people can't afford to give up work to look after a parent; others find themselves trapped in the 'tyranny-of-distance' situation. Some may be dealing with their partner's health problems or are disabled themselves, limiting their ability to help. Whatever your own circumstances, or your relationship with your parents, I sincerely hope some of the information in this book is relevant to your life.

With this in mind, you will find that the chapters in this book are organised in an order of growing awareness that parents might need help from you and your family, to providing information on helping them maintain their independence, through to leading active lives and eating well. Then, if larger problems do arise, the chapters in the second half of the book will help you tackle the more complex issues of waning independence, such as hospital admissions, moving, financial matters and the practical and emotional aspects of end of life issues. So whatever your situation, you should be able to find the information you need, with details of relevant organisations listed in a comprehensive Resources section at the end of the book.

There is, of course, a strong political element associated with the topic of growing old in the UK and obtaining state-funded help. I have tried to retain journalistic neutrality on this. Thankfully, the major issues of government funding and greater awareness of the needs of older people and their carers have started to creep up the political agenda. This is due in no small part to dedicated and unstinting lobbying from the relatively small number of charitable organisations involved (listed in the Resources section). So there could well be changes ahead that will improve things for many. But right now, it's fair to say that the more you can find out about what the situation involves, the better placed you will be to help your parents.

Let's face it, these are the people who nurtured and loved us when we were tiny and helpless; they gave us life itself. For that reason alone they deserve the very best we can possibly do for them.

Jacky Hyams

Note on benefit payments

Throughout the book current sums for benefits and allowances are quoted. Please note that while correct at the time of going to press, these are subject to change. Contact details of all the organisations involved are listed at the end of the book if you need to check for updates. (see Resources, pages 229–263).

1

Are there changes ahead?

Take a look in the mirror. Same familiar face, same blemishes, lines, marks of living and experience. Study it too hard and you might end up thinking of facelifts or expensive pots of miracle creams. Ignore the evidence and you might save yourself a lot of futile angst: nature will have its way. But whatever your feelings about the ageing process, it remains as inevitable as night follows day.

Today we often resist the very idea of ageing. Yet a hundred years ago, we accepted life's natural cycle. Back then, average life expectancy was around 45. It was accepted that young women often died in childbirth, teenage boys went off to fight, perhaps die, in wars. There was no NHS to cushion the blow of sickness, no counselling for bereavement or break-up, no pill option for women to limit families, no part-time jobs to pay for the holidays abroad or the new conservatory.

If people reached their sixties or beyond, there was no question of selling up to move to a retirement complex.

They remained where they lived, usually with their relatives. If they became frail or ill, their care was mostly the responsibility of their families – right to the end. And, of course, families were much larger: even when children left home to marry, they often remained near each other, sometimes in the same street.

Today the family unit is quite different: greater affluence and scientific advance have created a world where work now dominates everyday life in the way family once did. People frequently move cities or continents to live where their career takes them. It's taken for granted that families are scattered, often dotted across the country or across the globe.

Alongside these huge changes, we are living much longer. Current life expectancy is 86 for women, 76 for men and tipped to increase in the not too distant future.

So if we're contemplating a lifespan well beyond the allotted three score years and ten, what about our parents, the people who nurtured us and taught us about life? And, most importantly, how can we make sure that their old age is as comfortable, happy and secure as possible, so that their later years are not spent in some kind of miserable twilight dotage?

When is it time to step in and help?

It's likely that you don't even view your parents as 'old' in the traditional sense. Many of us have parents who may have technically retired some time ago, but remain fit, active, and independent irrespective of the calendar.

Today's seventy- and eightysomethings – and beyond – are often just as likely to be visiting grandchildren in Australia or surfing the net as they are to be sitting at home knitting or pottering around the allotment. Dramatic medical advances, better living conditions and improved economic circumstances have completely changed the lives of many people: elder independence has soared recently. Often, they're having as good a time – if not better – than the rest of us. Isn't that the way it ought to be?

Of course it is. The world is now everyone's oyster. But no matter how proudly independent our parents might be right now, what about the future? What happens if they start to lose some – or all – of that independence, either through failing health, circumstance – or just as a consequence of growing very old? How will they cope? And when do we, as their closest relatives, step in to help them continue to enjoy their lives and families, despite their frailties?

There are no clear answers. Judging precisely when it's time to step forward to help parents is not always clear-cut. You can't predict when it will happen, if, indeed, it will happen at all. And their wishes come first. You might already feel that they need to change things, downsize or move closer to you – and you may be right. But if they are independent and happy, they're not likely to want to relinquish any part of that independence in a hurry. Which makes a timetable for any major changes even more difficult to plan.

Because we are all unique in our genetic make-up, no geriatrician could ever tell you for sure exactly when your mum or dad will face deteriorating health and need much more of your help and support. It may never happen in quite the way you think – or it might happen quite soon.

Nature is even more capricious in the way it chooses to disable us as we age: the mind may stay alert and clear while the body deteriorates – or it might work the other way round. Some people suffer from memory problems and forgetfulness in their sixties, others remain sharp as a tack, playing bridge and finishing *The Times* crossword into their nineties. No two individuals will experience old age in exactly the same way. Which makes it doubly confusing to understand, let alone predict.

Don't expect to be asked to help

In most situations, you are probably going to have to rely on your own insights, observations and instincts to tell you when it's time to step in, rather than waiting for someone to say: 'Right, today's the day: your mum/dad/grandma/aunt needs more help from you.' And it's equally unlikely that your parents will suddenly opt to enlist your support; in most cases, they'd prefer to muddle along, telling you what you want to hear. So be warned: 'We're fine' can sometimes mean 'It's all a bit too difficult but there's no way we want to bother our kids.'

For most families, the realisation that a parent (or both parents) can't cope with everyday life at home any more comes as an unexpected shock: the big 'moment of truth' for many families follows a sudden emergency, often a fall at home, followed by a hospital stay, when it becomes evident that health problems mean that full independence is no longer on the agenda.

That sudden knowledge, in itself, is often difficult for younger family members to adjust to, let alone the realisation that they will be required to help their parents handle the changes ahead. Perhaps you have decided to be there to support your parents through any big changes. Yet you also need to be aware of the more subtle but hugely significant emotional aspects that accompany upheavals to daily routines. Most people have an enormous emotional attachment to their world. So handling those swift and irrevocable changes to what happens to your parents' home, their garden, their pets or their possessions requires considerable sensitivity on your part.

On the physical side, even doctors admit that dealing with the medical conundrums of old age can be complicated. One consultant told me: 'Geriatrics is a really challenging area of medicine because all the stuff you learn in medical school doesn't quite present itself in the same way in an elderly person: drugs work differently, everything is different. Even junior doctors and GPs sometimes find it too difficult to work with.'

Why advance homework is important

Because the ageing process is not easy to get to grips with, logic dictates you should prepare yourself. By being alert and informed, in advance, of what you should be looking out for in your parents' lives, you might be able to mitigate the effects of what lies ahead.

ADVANCE PLANNING CHECKLIST

✔ Start by researching the specific areas you think you might encounter down the line. For instance, if you think a move might be necessary eventually, use an Internet search to find out about alternatives, such as sheltered housing in their area (see Chapter 9, Moving, page 160). Keep printouts in a special file.

✔ Talk to other people about their elderly relatives. Communicating with others will play a big part in this situation; you could glean good ideas for your advance planning from colleagues or friends.

✔ Obtain Internet or printed information about local authorities, primary care trusts, local hospitals or GP surgeries. Most public authorities now produce a wide range of free literature with useful information and contact details for local elderly residents. These can be picked up in GP surgeries or local authority offices (see Chapter 6, Getting help, page 93).

✔ If possible, compile a file of personal information about your parents and keep it on your computer. Print out copies to hand to others, if necessary. You might not need it now but it could be handy in an emergency, especially if you live some distance away from your parents.

The file could include:
● Information about your parents' health (keep it brief, but include any regular medication details if you have them)

- National Insurance numbers
- Contact details for their GP, including an after-hours number, if possible
- Contact details for their local pharmacy
- Contact details for your parents' solicitor
- Names and phone numbers of neighbours or relatives nearby who are willing to help in an emergency
- Domestic details, i.e. landlord, housing association, mortgage lender, building society or bank account numbers
- Information on all sources of income, e.g. social security or state pension payments, private pension details, details of investments
- Documents relating to the home, e.g. insurance policies

You might not be able to obtain all this information: some parents' attitudes to their finances, for instance, can be reserved or defensive (see Chapter 11, Financial issues, page 196). But some detective work, especially in the area where your parents live, will usually produce quite a lot of information. (You may need to update the file from time to time, particularly if your parents move).

For further information, contact the National Centre for Independent Living (see Resources, page 229).

This 'homework' is something practical you can do at any time. What you can't do, of course, is pre-empt the unforeseen; nor can you be overprotective of an independent adult who might be quite resistant to the idea of you 'interfering' in their daily routines.

Nonetheless, if you can be attuned to pick up the small yet significant signs which indicate that a parent might need more help – or even requires immediate medical attention – it's an important practical step towards helping them.

Wanting to believe their repeated assurances that everything is 'fine' is perfectly natural. But sometimes you must look beyond the assurances, especially if the evidence before you is too compelling to be ignored . . .

THE SIGNS YOU CAN'T AFFORD TO IGNORE

- Tell-tale indications, in phone conversations, that a parent is becoming increasingly forgetful or less mentally alert

- Neglect of personal appearance – especially in someone who has always previously been scrupulous about their appearance

- A home that is not being looked after, especially a once-neat, tidy, spotless home that is clearly becoming chaotic

- Obvious confusion around money, e.g. bills not being paid. If you are repeatedly being told that money is going 'missing' or 'stolen', don't take it as gospel: the chances are, it's unlikely to be true. You will probably find the money hidden under a cushion or tucked away in a side drawer

- Behavioural changes that are out of character – and go on for some time, i.e. a fairly lively person becoming withdrawn or exceptionally quiet whenever you see them

- Repetitive behaviour that is also out of character, like baking cakes for a forthcoming event, noting it down, yet repeating the baking session afterwards

- Conversations in which they tell you they got 'lost' driving the car or while out walking

- A dramatic loss of weight since the last time you saw them. Look out for small signs, like a change in clothes size – or clothes that suddenly look far too big

- Food that would have normally been consumed but is clearly out of date. If there's lots of out-of-date food in the kitchen, mouldy bread or untouched milk, it could be they're forgetting to eat, especially if they live alone

- Medicine bottles that are out of date – or repeat prescriptions lying around

- A change in social habits, e.g. a marked reluctance to get out and about. Or frequent excuses not to see or visit people whose company they used to enjoy

- Letting unknown people, such as door-to-door sales-men, into the house, when they'd previously been diligent about security

- Strange smells of urine around the home. Incontinence problems are common in elderly people – but often very difficult for them to own up to

- Any mention of a fall – or more than one fall

- Signs of depression. This can be common in elderly people and can sometimes be a symptom of dementia

- Personality changes or difficulty in completing nor-mal household tasks (one or both of these could be signs of undiagnosed dementia)

- Poor appetite and sleeping problems (one or both of these could indicate either depression or early dementia)

You might not recognise any of these signs. There may be annoying little things that happen when you visit, like your mother's unfailing ability to lose her glasses or the shopping list, that might bother you. But such minor things are frequently just a consequence of getting older and more forgetful. So if you don't believe there's any real cause for concern, it may well be that things will stay that way for some time to come.

'Our decision was the right one'

Shirley, 94, lives alone in a small garden flat in north-west London. Her husband, George, died eight years ago. She worked as a part-time physio till she was 90 and is relatively fit and healthy.

Her three children, Dan, Ann and Jackie, live nearby, work full time and respect Shirley's iron will and independence. But they've had to be very subtle about helping her.

'We started noticing little things like her walking wasn't quite the same,' recalls Jackie. 'Then, she started having falls at home. It obviously cost her a lot to tell us.'

Shirley was still driving. 'The driving was getting dangerous. It had to stop. After a couple of months of gentle nagging, I started saying: "Oh, I'll drive." She was OK about that – she just didn't want to admit it was too hard.'

Crisis point came 18 months ago when Shirley fell over outside her home. 'She told us later that she immediately started shouting; luckily someone came to help quite quickly.'

Shirley had shattered the head of her femur. She needed two operations and spent three months in hospital. The doctors discovered angina – yet she refused an angioplasty.

'She said she didn't want to be fiddled with any more and we felt it was right to respect her wishes,' says Jackie. 'But how could she could go home again?'

Dan wanted Shirley to move to a care home; his sisters wanted her to try to stay independent at home. Shirley insisted she wanted to go home.

Back in her home, Shirley slowly regained her mobility. Now, the family continue to support her there, helped by a daily morning carer.

'She is getting frailer – her short-term memory is going and the angina makes her wheezy. But our decision was the right one,' says Jackie. *'Mum says the only way she'll leave her home is feet first. She's not maudlin – just very pragmatic. To her, that little bit of independence is very precious.'*

The changing relationship

Arming yourself with the right information is a practical exercise. But emotions are involved too. Your relationship with your parents is set to change if their independence does wane. And your own innermost feelings or concerns about growing old are bound to surface too (see Chapter 10, What about me?, page 181)

The parent–child relationship is unique in itself but, like all relationships, it has its nuances and complexities. Clearly a good, close relationship with parents is a wonderful plus in life, an enduring positive.

But not everyone looking to help or care for elderly parents is in this situation: there may be events or memories from the past that have hovered over the relationship or diluted any closeness. Perhaps you have always been much closer to one parent than the other, and have held back from much involvement in their lives over the years. Maybe your parents don't get on well with your partner, creating a less-than-easy atmosphere at family visits. Or your parents are quite a self-contained little unit – proud of the fact that they don't need any outside help.

Whatever the state of your relationship, if you are going be more involved with their lives – even if it is something as practical as helping move them – then it's important to accept that the relationship will change gear, because of the shift in responsibility. And if you've already consciously made a decision to help, any strong feelings about the past may need to be put to one side, for now at least, if you want to be supportive for the future.

Adjusting to change can be complex. If, for instance, you suddenly go from occasional phone calls and visits at Christmas to a two-hour visit, three times a week, there may be difficulties for everyone to overcome, simply because neither side is used to spending so much time in each other's company. It could take a month or two to adjust. By understanding that this transition might initially be difficult – and by explaining this to your parents, if you communicate well – any awkwardness can be smoothed over.

Coping with the frustrations

Emotionally you may experience initial frustration as you tackle the issues to do with helping a parent on a regular basis or spending more time with them. And it's quite likely you will get irritated by some of the smaller things that can crop up.

A friend's 86-year-old mother, living in a sheltered complex with a warden and an internal alarm in her flat, had an annoying habit of not replacing the receiver on the phone after my friend's daily midday call. This often resulted in frantic calls from my friend to the warden – or to the central call centre operating the electronic alarm system into her mother's flat.

Once the phone was back on the hook, my friend would end up yelling down the phone at her mother in sheer frustration. And her mother would be in tears.

Of course she was wrong to lose her temper. At 86, her mother didn't realise what she was doing. But after my friend had a long talk with a sympathetic professional, who explained that her reactions were natural but not to let her guilty feelings haunt her afterwards, the shouting and tears stopped.

It's wasted energy to let relatively minor upsets affect your relationship – or to worry afterwards about your reaction. What really matters is the bond between you, the love and care you have for your parents, not the tensions caring can create.

If a parent does accept your help and understands your desire to smooth the path for them, as it were, your relationship can only strengthen. Even if mum or dad (or both) goes on to become heavily dependent on your presence, it won't lessen or diminish the love you have for each other.

And rather than feel uneasy about the changes, look at it this way: once, they were the care givers, the nurturers when you were tiny. Now you're there to do the same for them. Instinct alone tells us that caring for parents you love is a very natural process and just nature's way of rounding things off.

The time-poor society

But what if you can't be there for them most of the time? The work factor, so dominant in our lives, truncates our existence – and frequently makes any kind of continuous visiting an exercise in planning and prioritising.

As an only child without offspring, I initially saw myself as being hugely disadvantaged in that there were no other close family members to support me when it came to helping my mother. Over time, I changed my view. Even in the largest, most caring families, many people are at some kind of logistical or practical disadvantage when it comes to being there to help on a regular basis.

Maybe you're still working full time, your partner is working too – and one or more of your children remains at home. So time spent helping your parents has to be fitted around the rest of your life. This is fine if you live near your parents, but not so good if you live even an hour or more away and work long hours in a stressful environment while your partner is equally preoccupied with work – or even their own parents' problems. Like it or not, many of us now live in a hideously 'time-poor' environment.

Then, of course, there is the tyranny of distance. Your parents may have retired and moved to live in the sun. Or to Scotland or Cornwall, making regular visits restricted – and stressful. We may live in a small island but it's incredibly overcrowded: a weekend's long motorway drive, a packed train ride or a cross-country coach trip don't exactly make for a relaxing prelude to a visit you've planned for weeks.

And even if your infrequent visits make you increasingly aware that something positive has to be done to help your parents before disaster strikes, how do you approach tackling it if you can't pop in frequently?

Why the phone is so important

In such a situation, regular phone calls are your key resource. If you are really worried, upping the ante on the calls – i.e. daily, rather than once a week – is sensible, especially if you can make the call at the same time each day, perhaps in the morning before going to work.

Organising something as simple as a daily phone call with military-style planning might sound odd. But the pay-off, in many cases, is reassurance – for everyone. Keeping the flow of communication going will help considerably, provided you are realistic about what you can contribute if time is really tight (see Chapter 2, Family relationships, page 23).

'I wish I wasn't so far away'

Beatty, 93, was widowed five years ago. She lives alone in the small house in Kent she has lived in for 50 years. Her daughter Jane, 62, is a 45-minute drive away. Her other daughter, Sonya, 60, has lived in Australia for over 20 years.

'Mum has always been an independent, active sort of person,' recalls Sonya. 'She travelled regularly, well into her eighties.'

When her father died, Jane hoped Beatty would move into her large house with a separate granny flat, purchased years before with Beatty in mind. Jane and her partner work full time. But this way, they could keep an eye on Beatty.

But Beatty refused. So the sisters devised an alternative plan: 'Jane visits Mum once a week, does the shopping and laundry, checks everything and rings her every night. I ring from Australia every morning at exactly the same time. I fly over to stay with Mum twice a year,' explains Sonya.

Beatty has remained physically active. But her mind is deteriorating. She often insists that money is being stolen from her – in fact, Jane recently found a large wad of cash hidden in a bedroom cupboard. Two home carers visit daily to help. But her daughters are worried.

'Mum needs to be somewhere safer with people around but she refuses to live with Jane,' sighs Sonya. 'She did say, for the first time, that she wants to move to sheltered housing. So we're looking for a sheltered flat for her.

'The way we've shared this works. But in my heart of hearts, I wish I could be here for her all the time. Jane thinks it's hard, doing the domestic stuff. But it's just as hard sitting by the phone in Australia, knowing that if she does need me urgently, I'm over 24 hours away.'

CHECKLIST: IF YOU CARE – BUT CAN'T BE THERE

✔ For your own peace of mind, try to set up some sort of plan. It might mean changing or amending your normal schedule for visits. If you can't do that, negotiate by phone with outside help – or other family members who are willing to help.

✔ If you do live a long way away, e.g. Australia or the US, recognise the limitations of distance. Getting frustrated or angry about the situation won't help. If there's no possibility of you moving back to be closer, then accept things as they are – not how you wish they would be.

✔ Try to replicate what you'd do if you lived nearby by phoning regularly, at a set time. Your parents may remember when you're due to ring. Or they may forget that you ring regularly. But the sound of your voice is always reassuring.

✔ Send photographs frequently. If parents are computer literate for emailed photos, all the better. Aim to show them, through regular and frequent communication, that you're still a strong presence in their lives.

✔ Maintain contact with other family members who see your parents regularly. And don't be scared to contact them out of the blue if you're worried about something.

✔ Don't be daunted by the changes that may come about without you being there, e.g. if your parents move house.

✔ Try to deal with it all in bite-sized pieces, rather than trying to do everything all at once. Panicking and flapping doesn't help anyone.

2

Family relationships

W e've witnessed astonishing social change since the day our parents watched proudly as we took our first wobbly steps in the world. And nowhere has this change been more noticeable than within the family unit.

Perhaps your own background is the traditional nuclear family: two parents, two children. Fast forward half a century or so to a very different family landscape: divorce and remarriage are normal, as is the increase in single-parent families and the blended family, where couples (or single parents) raise offspring from different partners under one roof.

Adoption, once a secretive process, is now widely accepted, with more people seeking out their birth parents than ever before. And there's a broader acceptance of same-sex relationships. Nowadays the very word 'family' can mean a totally different set of permutations of the traditional idea.

Your parents might have divorced years ago. One (or both) might have remarried – and created a whole new family, including step-grandchildren. Perhaps one divorced parent remains alone, not fully accepting the change in circumstances, and is already more dependent on their children: many family relationships change considerably after remarriage. Or a parent might be widowed. Any of these situations can bring their own set of problems or sensitivities.

Why family matters so much

But while society may have readily absorbed these huge changes in our family relationships, when individual concerns turn to the welfare of elderly relatives, our relationship with siblings and other relatives becomes crucial.

Ideally, your own children share the love and concern you have for your parents and fully understand that, in some cases, your mum or dad may have made real sacrifices to give you the life you have today. Moreover, as grandparents they might have made a big contribution to the welfare and upbringing of your kids. In that case, your children will instinctively understand why you want – or need – to be there for their grandparents.

But we don't live in an ideal world. We all know families who are close knit, loving and eager to help with parental needs at the drop of a hat – but for most, it's not as simple as that. Life today for many families has evolved into a series of compromises, in order to fit in all the different work and domestic demands.

Emotionally, we may want to move heaven and earth to do what we can for our parents. Yet on a practical level we often need all the help from others that we can muster.

For this reason alone, a contribution from the rest of the family can make an enormous difference to your parents' well-being. By sharing care, in any way, everyone wins. And we're not talking about huge sacrifices either: it's often quite small gestures that count.

For instance, if a parent is in their eighties or nineties and not quite as active as they were, an unexpected visit from a grown-up grandson, or a close relative not seen for years, might mean the visitor making a detour, for a few hours, out of a packed itinerary. Yet that one thoughtful act can give great pleasure. If a few photos are taken too, then there it is cemented in time, a bit of family history to recall, a treasured few hours to enjoy.

Why grandchildren are so important

Adult grandchildren may have their own lives to pursue, their own family to bring up, or live in a different part of the world, making regular contact unlikely. But if they live reasonably close to your parents, their presence can make a huge difference.

Grandchildren are the family jewels, in a sense. In so many ways, they are the vital link between the generations. If your children are close to your parents, the richness and value of the relationship has already added much to your parents' lives – and given your children a strong sense of identity and stability. As a grandparent yourself, you will understand this perfectly. And if your parents are no longer physically capable of looking after your own grandchildren in the way they did your kids, being around their tiny great-grandchildren, whenever it can be arranged, is still a tremendous bonus. So encouraging such visits is always worthwhile. It might mean a few extra phone calls or emails. But your parents can only gain from seeing them.

Look at it this way: life may have changed for them suddenly, with more restriction in what they can do. Yet witnessing the early days of those small lives that are so closely linked to theirs is more than just a comfort – it reinforces their sense of well-being and continuity, the part of them that will live on long after they've gone.

The significance of the grandparent relationship is often overlooked. Yes, they are fantastic babysitters – the biggest providers of childcare in the UK: 13 million grandparents currently care for their offspring's children on a regular basis. And when grandparents have the time and space to nurture their grandchildren as youngsters, there's an instinctive bonding process that endures into adulthood.

Perhaps you saw more of each other when they were younger and then either you or your parents moved away. Don't believe for a moment that the distance might have created an emotional barrier. For where such relationships are good, they tend to stay good, especially if strong bonds were developed in early childhood. And geographical separation nowadays is much easier to bridge with technology – mobile phones, text messages, web cameras. Even if your parents aren't technologically clued up, low-cost, long-distance phone calls and regular cards and photos in the post will do a great deal to keep the relationship alive and thriving.

The 'emotional sandwich'

But where does that leave you? Emotionally, you could be caught in the crossfire because you're having to juggle the conflicting needs of family and work commitments, trying to fit everything in, so that parents don't lose out.

As someone who has run their office from home for years, free of the rigid 9–5 timetable, I've lost count of the times I've given thanks for my self-employed status when I've had to drop everything to be there for my mum. Being a home worker offers considerable flexibility when you're juggling family needs too. Part-time work also helps. But if, like many, you work full time and commute, it is that much harder to juggle all your responsibilities.

Those responsibilities might also mean having grown-up children still living at home. Nowadays, offspring don't always leave home at 18, partly because housing in the UK is costly but also because people tend to marry much later (the average age of marriage is now 28–30).

Maybe they're still studying. Or they remain at home but outside the workforce, a sore point for some families and often an emotional strain for everyone in the household, financial implications included.

Whatever the circumstances, if they're still living under your roof, you'd be an unusual parent if you didn't still feel responsible for them. And there's your partner to consider too, with their own work responsibilities, let alone their concerns for their own parents.

Rest assured, if you feel overwhelmed by balancing the need to be there for your family as well as for your parents, you are not alone. In emotional terms, many people helping elderly parents find themselves in this situation, caught in a 'sandwich' of conflicting feelings, split between worrying how they will manage to juggle it all –and feeling guilty that they can't do more because they have too much on their plates.

Coping with conflicting needs

So how do you handle this balancing act? These ideas should help you:

- Acknowledge the fact that you have certain limitations: you can't be all things to everyone all the time.
- If you work full time, accept that you will definitely need to enlist help and support from others.
- Communicate with your family. Discuss it properly with your partner and children. Tell them that, in the short term, you'll need more help or support from them on the home front because of what's happening with your parents. Explain that their extra input will free you up to have more time for your parents.
- Remember, support doesn't have to be huge. It can come in many small ways. By asking a number of people for a little bit of help rather than one person for a lot, things could be a bit easier.
- Enlist help from close friends in small ways. For instance, a friend might be happy to collect something for you locally or drive you short distances, if necessary, if they know it helps you.
- If house cleaning is a major issue at home, consider hiring a once-weekly cleaner, even for a few months, if

you can afford it. It can buy you two or three hours' freedom a week when you really need it (see Chapter 3, Maintaining independence, page 39).

Workplace tactics

You might need to ask for time off work. It could be part of your annual leave, though some large companies are willing to grant employees compassionate leave in certain circumstances. Contact your human resources department to find out what options are available.

Employers are increasingly aware that their employees' elderly relatives might need help: some employers, like British Gas, BT and Asda, have already adopted specific carer-friendly working practices. And because many people have been forced, in the past, to give up work to care for elderly parents, the new Work and Families Act (in force since April 2007) gives any employee caring for an elderly relative the legal right to request flexible working. So your work routine could be altered to fit in with your personal commitments.

Your colleagues are probably already aware of the increasing demands on your time; if you're open about the situation – without going into too much detail – people are more likely to be understanding. Other colleagues might be experiencing the same situation with their elderly relatives. This can be mutually beneficial. There's no harm in sharing your experiences or feelings about your respective situations outside office hours.

As for your employers, make it clear that you intend to carry on doing the job to the best of your ability – but explain that right now, you will be juggling your commitments. And when you've done that, stop worrying about how you'll cope with the job if such-and-such happens to your parents. In this situation, a step-by-step, one-day-at-a time approach is much more sensible – and manageable – than living on the edge of a 'what if' emotional volcano.

Remember too that while you may be worrying endlessly about juggling everything, your parents are probably far more realistic about what you can do than you realise.

Your parents know you don't have unlimited amounts of time at your disposal; if you do tell them that you are trying to create more time to be with them, with limitations, the chances are they'll understand and accept you're doing what you can.

GETTING EVERYONE INVOLVED

- If you're a grandparent yourself, consider your links with other grandparents within the family set-up: if you have built up a good rapport over the years, you may find they are more understanding and supportive than you imagined.

- Encourage your parents, and other elderly close relatives, to consider using the Internet and/or learning to text message: it's a wonderful way of communicating with younger members of the family.

- If your children or grandchildren travel frequently, encourage them to send regular postcards to grand-parents and elderly relations. Older people still view the postal system as a primary means of communication. For the price of a stamp, they receive a pleasant surprise in the post. It also gives them a chance to communicate back, even to say: 'When are you coming to see us?'

- Ask one of your children (or do it yourself if you have time) to research and draw up a family tree. In families where there are lots of divorces and remarriages, this is a wonderful way for everyone to know where they fit into the family and a great focus for your parents' input when you visit. It makes them feel important – and needed.

- If other younger relatives seem unwilling to visit your parents, understand that lack of exposure to elderly people can lead to misunderstandings. They might assume, for instance, that communication with your parents might be difficult or embarrassing. Make it clear that your mum or dad is just as much the person they always were – just a bit older.

- Encourage your children, whatever their age, to get involved in domestic activity in and around your parents' home: cooking, gardening, shopping, helping round the house, collecting prescriptions. Your parents are far more likely to accept this kind of help from them than from a stranger.

Everybody loves good neighbours

Neighbours are, of course, another vital source of communication and support in all our lives. So often it's a two-way sharing street: you help them out by caring for their cat when they go away; they turn up trumps for you when you lock yourself out or have a minor domestic disaster.

At its very best, in a good neighbourly relationship you start out sharing local or domestic concerns – and end up as really good friends.

When it comes to parents living some distance away from their family, however, it's slightly different. Your parents' neighbours may be good friends to them and an invaluable source of support. Yet no matter how good they've been in the past, you should not take them for granted or put too much pressure or responsibility on them, especially if your parents' needs change dramatically.

If you don't live nearby but become seriously concerned about your mum or dad's increasing frailty, by all means discuss this with their closest neighbours by phone. Make it clear you appreciate everything they've done in the past. And tell them they can contact you, at any time, if they are worried about anything involving your parents. If it's appropriate, give them your work number too. Ask if you can ring them, if you have any concerns.

But do be aware that leaning too heavily on neighbours or letting them bear the burden of the day-to-day difficulties your parents might be experiencing is an imposition. They may be helpful and caring neighbours, but they are not unpaid care workers. Too much responsibility can make them feel put upon, especially if they are elderly too.

Should you give your parents' neighbours keys to their home? In rural or suburban areas, it's quite common for one or two trusted neighbours to have a set of other neighbours' keys. But in a big city, where security fears abound, some people resist the idea.

The sensible approach is to ask your parents. If they strongly object to anyone else having keys – and you suspect this is largely due to reluctance to give up their independence – be discreet. Leave things as they are. But if it helps your own peace of mind, give a copy of their door key discreetly to one trusted neighbour. Make it clear it's only for an emergency and ask them to ring you before using it. That key may never be used. But it is a safeguard.

Long-distance siblings

Maybe you have brothers or sisters who live abroad. They might have lived overseas for years – and at times, contact might have been intermittent. Some families do remain quite detached in this way, until concern for elderly parents dictates a need to talk about the situation.

As we've already noted, the distance won't have affected close family relationships. You probably won't even have to ask for help; they'll move heaven and earth to be there when they can be – and if they can't get there, they'll use all means of communication at their disposal to support you.

However, you might find yourself struggling to comprehend a lack of concern from some long-distance siblings. Particularly if contact has been very limited. Or there's been a family rift.

Coping with rifts

When it comes to any kind of rift or argument between you and your siblings, wherever they live, it's fair to say that both parties should be sensible and adult enough to put the rift or argument aside – in the common interest of helping their parents. Hanging on to that resentment over past differences won't help anyone.

But not everyone sees it this way. For instance, you might approach a sibling living abroad in the spirit of reconciliation, only to be rebuffed or ignored. For some people, it is easier to put family business to one side when living thousands of miles away.

When this does happen, it may hurt like hell – but you need to focus on priorities and not get sidetracked by negatives. Getting upset with close relatives who aren't as concerned as you are is pretty much a wasted emotion. In a situation that might already be frustrating, letting your feelings get the better of you when you're faced with indifference – or even silence – isn't advisable.

Resist the temptation to let rip over the phone. Discuss it with one or two people close to you, e.g. your children or partner. Make one more polite attempt at communication if you must. But if they don't want to get involved, accept it. You need all your emotional energy to focus on what you can do, rather than on other people's issues.

Here are some other strategies to help cope with conflict with relatives:

- If someone says something hurtful, try telling them in a non-confrontational way, e.g. 'That really hurt' or 'I was really upset when you said that.' It may not change anything, but you've aired your feelings.

- If that doesn't work and the same relative continues to upset you by their behaviour or attitude, remove yourself from their firing line if you can. Don't give them any more opportunities to upset you.

- If you're upset about a sibling who has never shown much interest in helping your parents over the years, try writing a letter which you never send. Put all your feelings into it. Then destroy it by burning it or tearing it into tiny pieces. By throwing it away, you may deal with some of your hurt and can then concentrate on the present situation.

- Consider a person's motivation if they keep saying upsetting or bitchy things. They may have a completely separate agenda. For instance, they may be trying to get back at other siblings through you. Don't let their behaviour deflect you from what you're trying to do.

- Focus on the positive. Is there a relative who does not live nearby who shows genuine interest in the situation? Knowing you can ring or email them regularly may meet an unspoken need in you to share your concern with someone in the family.

Going it alone

Maybe you don't have any family help to enlist. Maybe you're widowed or divorced, without children. Or, like me, an only child without offspring. You may have a partner who spends large amounts of time working away from home.

All of these situations are emotionally challenging – and, in a sense, quite isolating. Again, your best step is to enlist emotional support by talking to others. It might be a sympathetic friend or neighbour in a similar situation – but if that isn't an option, you may have to seek out help elsewhere. The worst thing you can do is clam up and not speak to anyone.

My own experience when my mother started to become more needy and frail was unhappy and confusing. By nature an outgoing person, I initially found close friends were sympathetic and helpful when I shared my feelings. But I expected too much and made far too many panicky phone calls, especially when she was in hospital. I felt quite helpless. In my frustration I became demanding – and angry. I wanted their help, but nothing they could say was reassuring enough. How could it be?

Long-term friendships were damaged, though most weren't ruined for good. Through my local authority, Camden, I managed to get some free one-hour counselling sessions. And this did help – the counsellor was non-judgemental and made it clear that my feelings of guilt, confusion and fear were a very human response to an all-too-common life crisis.

Then I had to cancel appointments, because of the other demands on my time, and lost the right to further sessions. But I'd learned a hard lesson: in my panic, I didn't stop to think of the effect of my behaviour – and how upsetting my anger was to friends who had already lost parents or were struggling with their own problems.

Talk it through

Unless you live in a very remote area, there should be some form of local support within your community to let you talk about how you feel about the changes in your parents' lives. Your local authority is a good starting point. Or local carers' organisations, charities, church or religious groups might be able to point you in the right direction for group counselling or therapy sessions.

If you'd prefer one-to-one sessions, free NHS counselling is not easily obtainable and waiting lists are months long in some areas. Your GP is more likely to be offer you drugs for anxiety or depression, which might not be appropriate. If you can afford private counselling, expect to pay £35–£50 per session, depending on location. But whatever your circumstances, this is not a time to bottle things up.

For further information, contact the British Association for Counselling and Psychotherapy or Relate (see Resources, pages 229–30).

Why plans matter

Consider the way you look forward to a holiday. Or a visit to a close friend you haven't seen for ages. We all need something special to look forward to, probably more so when we're much older. However, when we get caught up with concern for parents, seeking practical solutions for their everyday welfare, it can be quite easy to overlook the importance of their social life, which ensures they can look ahead to a special event or outing.

Making plans for birthday celebrations, family gatherings or anniversaries will take up extra time. But the better you plan – and discuss those plans with your parents so that they know what's happening – the more cheerful their perspective, especially if they're no longer organised enough to plan ahead themselves.

Birthday celebrations, especially big ones, do merit quite a lot of thought. The more help you have, the easier it is. And if other family members are willing to put that extra bit of imagination into the planning, there's every chance that everyone involved, especially your parents, will really enjoy the event itself – and look back on it with extreme pleasure.

Don't overlook the value of documenting it: photos or camcorder home movies will give endless delight to your parents long after the event.

PLANNING THE GOOD TIMES

- The phone is a lifeline for elderly people, especially if they're virtually housebound. If you can't pop in regularly, establish a regular routine for phone calls.

  Try to ring at the same time each day at a time that suits everyone. Someone living alone might also find it more reassuring to get a regular evening call.

- Make time to think about small surprises: a bunch of flowers when you turn up or an inexpensive but unexpected gift is a simple way to show you care.

And presents are often appreciated more than you might imagine.

- For birthday celebrations or big anniversaries, find a decent hotel near your parents' home so that family members can stay overnight without crowding your parents' home. If the budget runs to it, have the party there too, thus avoiding family squabbles about cooking or clearing up.

- Use those family gatherings as a chance to celebrate your parents' achievements while they're still here. We tend to use funerals to celebrate a life but why not tell your parents at least once, in full view of everyone they care for: 'You're great and we think the world of you'?

- Celebrate and encourage reminiscence. Get one or both parents to record their life experiences on tape (you can set it up for them if they can't do it). The result is a permanent store of memories of their life – in their own words.

3

Maintaining independence

In ten years' time there will be more people over 65 than under 25 living in the UK. And many of those over-65s will still be around in their eighties – and well beyond. Were you to ask each one how much help they think they might need from others in later years, most would say they don't want anyone helping them, thank you. They can manage quite well on their own. After all, who wants to end up depending on other people?

It's an unusual person who relinquishes their independence easily. Of course, we depend on other people for our emotional needs. We need to know we're loved, cared for, needed, wanted – and approved of. Those emotional ties with those closest to us help make us tick as human beings.

However, we're all quite different in how much we depend on others on a practical or daily level; individual personalities and circumstances are so diverse. If you've opted to be there to help your parents in any way you can, if you're fortunate, your parents will be quite happy for you to step in and take more responsibility for their well-being.

But for many families, the problem is that around the time when it starts to be obvious that more help is needed, the parents insist they don't want it.

The idea of any kind of change involving help from others, particularly for those whose lives are quite separate from their children, might be anathema to some parents. How often do you hear: 'I don't want to be a burden on anyone'? Mostly, they really mean it.

So if you are struggling to understand why your mum or dad is being so obstinate or intransigent, think on this: you'll probably be the same when you're older. Even as we slow down physically and mentally we still assume we can somehow cope – because we nearly always have. Independence is something we take for granted, even if it may be clear to an outsider that our bodies are failing us or slowing us down.

Getting the balance right

How can you balance your parents' determination to stay independent with your desire to help them?

First of all, get your priorities straight. You can't barge in and take over. No matter how chaotic their lives may seem to you, your parents retain the right to make their own decisions.

In some circumstances, e.g. severe dementia, that might not be the case (see Chapter 7, Key health issues, page 123). But whatever you do to help your parents, you should not attempt to diminish their sense of control over their lives. Bullying your way through is not an option. Unless their health or safety at home is clearly in jeopardy, their wishes still have to come first.

Yes, you argue, but the house is a mess. Repairs haven't been done for ages, the garden's neglected and the place looks terrible, even shabby – when it used to be spotless. Yet whenever you venture to mention getting more help or changing things, your parents insist that all is well – they don't want anyone else 'interfering' around the place.

How can you tackle this situation? First of all, recognise what is really going on: it's probably alien to their nature to admit they need more help. They have their pride and their dignity; if these can't be maintained, it could have a fundamental effect on their confidence to manage the rest of their lives.

Understand their perspective

For your part, you can't really force your expectations or ideas of what is acceptable in everyday life on to an older generation.

It's easy to forget that people in their seventies or eighties weren't brought up in an all-powerful consumer society as we were.

Many of us view things like cars, mobile phones, central heating, computers, washing machines and dishwashers as essentials. Life without them, we believe, is virtually unimaginable, a step back to the Dark Ages.

Yet many older people won't see it that way. They lived through the Second World War when life's basics, like food, clothing and fuel, were rationed. And 'making do' back then was a virtue, even an achievement. It's difficult for us to make sense of this because we haven't experienced life in this way.

Dirt and chaos aside, a home lacking in what we consider to be 'essentials' might easily be perfectly acceptable to an elderly relative. Healthcare professionals say they encounter this problem all the time. Caring families struggle with the idea that elderly parents won't accept any form of domestic help, or even gifts like a small microwave oven, to ease their life. In most cases, parents truly believe such things are unnecessary, or frivolous. They can manage, they say. And that's what they do.

Difficult as it is, try to acknowledge this. Your view of your parents' environment or possessions may not, in any way, match theirs. You might believe their home is full of clutter and junk that needs throwing out; they might treasure their belongings, no matter how battered or worthless they seem to you. And when you treasure something, it's hurtful, even threatening to be told it must be discarded because it's useless. So you really have to try to look beyond your own values when considering the state of your parents' home. They're probably deeply attached to it – and perfectly happy there – whatever it looks like.

Tackling domestic issues

You might see a dirty, untidy place in which a weekly cleaner for just a few hours could make a difference. Or a once well-tended garden that badly needs some TLC. Of course domestic help, if affordable, is an intelligent

solution in a home where someone is struggling to maintain order, especially if it's a family home that needs quite a
bit of looking after.

Experts say that good help in the home can also make a
huge difference to older people's overall well-being in the
long term. It frees them up to enjoy other things, and helps
them enjoy existing independence. But for many older
women, their life's work has been entirely domestic – keeping the home spick and span, supporting their husband,
raising the family. It's their identity, their role in life.
Giving up even part of that can, for some, be quite scary,
amounting to a loss of control over everything they cher-
ish. So understanding their perspective might help prevent
tearful arguments and upsets when you suggest getting
more help.

The following ideas might help you overcome your parents' reluctance to accepting help at home:

- If the home is really neglected, don't barge in with: 'I'm
  getting a cleaner, you can't cope any more.' Float the
  idea first. Say you understand why they want to keep
  doing their own housework. But make it clear you want
  to find a way to help them keep it clean.

- Try saying you think the time they spend cleaning or
  cooking could be used more efficiently sometimes;
  perhaps if you or your siblings were more involved you
  could spend more time together. This involvement could
  extend to offering to prepare meals for them when
  visiting.

- You could also enlist an enthusiastic family member,
  perhaps a grown-up grandchild with an interest in
  cooking, to prepare a special family meal. This may

involve some planning, but parents are unlikely to reject the idea.

- Get the man of the house involved. If he's fit and she's less robust, perhaps he can prepare the occasional meal, or help clean or shop. If his involvement in domestic chores has been limited, use some tact. You might hear: 'Your mother won't hear of it'. But you could find he's up for it.

- Your parents might worry that a stranger coming in to clean or garden might somehow 'take control'. Ease this fear by offering personally to find someone who might be suitable – and, if possible, to be there to help interview them.

- If the above tactic works and they seem to like a prospective cleaner or gardener, suggest an initial 'trial' session. That way, at least you'll achieve something.

- If none of these approaches works, attempt a quick tidy up of the kitchen or an especially untidy room when you visit. Or offer to help clean out a drawer, a cupboard – or even cut the grass.

Hiring domestic help

If they do agree to outside help, unless your parents already know someone locally, the best way to source a reliable cleaner or gardener is to ask around locally for recommendations or check local newspaper classified ads. You could also look at notice-boards in local newsagents or post offices. Using a domestic agency or industrial home-cleaning service for routine housework isn't always advisable because they are quite pricey; such resources are more useful for a major one-off cleaning job, e.g. when moving house.

Once you find someone suitable, always request a reference (get phone numbers of people you can ring and check yourself) and make it clear at interview stage what is expected – and what will be paid. Never hire anyone for your parents without meeting them first, unless it's a local person they already know.

Pay varies according to area. Expect to pay £5–£8 per hour for a cleaner, £8–£15 per hour for a gardener, depending on whether you live in the country (lower figure) or city (higher figure).

Food shopping options

You could suggest taking your parents out to a nearby restaurant as a treat, making sure you choose a place that serves the kind of food they enjoy. This could give you a chance to open up a conversation afterwards about food shopping, if it's obvious this is becoming a problem. Perhaps one parent has recently stopped driving or a recently widowed parent has never driven at all.

There may be neighbours who are willing to help by driving them to the shops sometimes, if you or your siblings are short of time. But another idea is to use a local taxi service for weekly shopping trips (see Chapter 5, Encouraging an active life, page 85). Local firms often rely on elderly passengers for a major part of their business; you may even be able to negotiate a small discount for regular trips.

Ordering the weekly supermarket shop over the Internet has simplified much of the shopping/delivery dilemma. Your parents might not be computer literate or initially willing to consider doing their food shopping this way, but you can offer to order a 'sample' weekly shop for them online, for home delivery. Explain that you'll pay with your credit card and they can reimburse you in cash later. If they like the idea and you can fit their weekly order in with your own timetable, that might ease their shopping burden.

Alternatively, large supermarket chains like Sainsbury's will take phone orders and deliver within 48 hours. There is a delivery charge (around £5), so this might not suit everyone.

When a partner won't accept change

Sometimes one parent is quite willing to accept outside help while the other is stubbornly resistant. Here again, it helps to understand the emotions fuelling this kind of resistance to modifying their way of life:

- Shock: that things are having to change at all
- Fear: what will the future hold if we let this happen?
- Anger: why is this happening at all?

These are very powerful emotions. As a consequence, admitting that changes are occurring becomes difficult for some people; they flatly refuse to acknowledge alternatives. That way, for them, change does not exist. And they still feel 'safe'.

Overcoming the effect of these complex emotions is rarely simple. But you should try to communicate your concerns. Try asking the parent who won't accept any changes how things will be for the other person, i.e. their partner, if they can't get any help? Will they feel guilty about not doing the things they've always done? Ask too: what is there to gain by not acknowledging the changes and accepting the extra help?

These are pointed questions. But the end justifies the means: by approaching the issue in subtle, non-threatening terms you might be able to move things forward. But don't steamroll or try to blackmail your parents into accepting changes. The result is likely to be even more resistance.

Why advance checking is useful

If you find yourself stuck in a situation in which your parents are ambling along, refusing any help, hanging on to their waning independence, with no real direct threat to their welfare, it's still sensible to have some sort of plan for what might lie ahead. Knowing where to go or whom to contact in an emergency is always useful. Especially if you don't live close by and may have to organise help from a distance.

Start this plan by looking at the main sources of assistance in the home, other than hiring a local cleaner or gardener. These sources are: voluntary organisations, i.e. charities, local authority funded assistance; or help from private agencies.

Help from a local authority

While some local authorities offer schemes for helping elderly people at home with shopping, light housework and personal care, the process for obtaining such help is quite complicated and unless your parents have a very limited income, it is not free of charge – or even available in every area (see Chapter 6, Getting help, page 93).

On the positive side, if there are concerns about the idea of letting a total stranger into the home, regulation of employees working with the elderly in their own homes has been tightened up: all agencies offering paid-for help from home-care staff are now legally required to register with the Care Quality Commission and to conform to its minimum standards. Private-agency employees must also be registered with the General Social Care Council (for further information, see Resources, page 230). If you do access outside home-care help, the risk of the wrong person coming into your parents' home is much lower.

Help from a voluntary organisation

Many older people will accept help from a well-known, trusted voluntary organisation, simply because they feel more comfortable accepting help from an outsider, rather than their family. But in the main, this type of help is short term, usually following a crisis, i.e. 4–6 weeks. And it might not be available in your parents' area.

Organisations like Age Concern and the Red Cross offer some elder home-care services, so as part of your advance game plan, contact their local branches to find out what might be available, what it costs and the circumstances in which your parents might be eligible for this extra help.

The Red Cross, in particular, provide excellent short-term support for older people, involving assistance with shopping or simple domestic tasks. It is usually provided after a hospital stay or following an accident in the home, e.g. after a person breaks a limb. The service is not means tested but it is quite limited. For further information, see Resources, page 231.

If you do not live nearby and have one parent living alone in a reasonably sized house or flat with a spare bedroom, you could also check in advance with the charity Homeshare International. Homeshare run a scheme for elderly people who need extra help with tasks and chores because they are having difficulty living alone. The scheme matches the person with someone in their twenties, either a student or someone in full-time work, willing to provide help and reassurance at night, in exchange for free accommodation.

People are carefully matched to ensure compatibility. The schemes are only available in London, Oxford, Bristol and West Sussex at present, although there are plans to expand it further. Charges apply in London only; these are negotiable, depending on income. For further information, see Resources, page 231.

Help from a private agency

For private agencies providing assistance with personal care (i.e. washing and dressing) or live-in and nursing care, compile a list of suitable agencies in your parents' area by contacting the United Kingdom Homecare Association. The Care Quality Commission will also provide useful details of accredited agencies.

The cost of services provided by private agencies varies a great deal; there are no set fees. If you have time to contact a few and ask what they offer, the details could be useful later. For further information, see Resources, page 232.

Are your parents safe?

There are things you might be able to do yourself to increase your parents' comfort and safety around their home – and prevent unnecessary accidents.

SAFETY CHECKLIST

✔ Are they wearing the right kind of footwear? Comfortable, well-fitting flat shoes with non-slip soles are best. Scuffed down-at-heel slippers or Dad's ancient gardening shoes should be binned. New slippers should have proper backs; avoid slip-ons.

✔ Look carefully at floor coverings. Rugs that slide easily or are loose are dangerous. If possible, remove them.

✔ Is the central heating boiler working properly? Does it need servicing? Is the thermostat easy to use?

✔ Is the bathroom safe? Consider safety aids like rubber mats or extra rails to limit chances of slipping. Is the toilet seat too low? They may need a 'booster' seat – unattractive but better than an ambulance turning up because they're stuck on the loo seat.

✔ Are there any steps or stairs without handrails? If so, get handrails fitted. Steps and stairs are the most common places for falls.

✔ Do they use the loo frequently at night? Is there a light nearby? And check the route they take for any safety hazards, e.g. trailing wires, especially on stairs.

✔ Check the bed. Is it easy to get in and out of? Is the mattress old and in need of replacement? Is there a bed-side light so that when they do get up, they're less likely to trip?

✔ Check furniture. Can it be rearranged so they can move around more easily? Are the armchairs suitable? Squishy sofas are useless for older people who might have trouble getting up. The best type of chair, depending on the person's height, is one with armrests on either side so they don't have to struggle to stand up.

✔ Are there steps outside the house? Get a can of white paint and mark the edges by painting a white strip along the edge, to help visibility.

✔ Examine garden surfaces. Remove fallen leaves from drives and pathways. Consider repairing or treating slippery, uneven surfaces like mossy paths or cracked concrete.

✔ If they are keen on gardening, are window boxes or tubs at the right height so they can still enjoy using a trowel?

✔ Do a lighting check. Dim lights cause accidents. Replace bulbs with energy-saving ones that don't need frequent replacement.

✔ If they're driving, can they park safely close to home?

Homecraft Rolyan supply a wide range of items, including adapted kitchenware and specially angled cutlery to help elderly or disabled people. For further information, see Resources, page 232.

Security concerns

One major concern for families is personal safety. The more secure your parents feel in their home, the more their sense of independence is boosted.

If you can visit your parents' local police station, the crime prevention officer should be able to give you useful advice about security in the home.

Fire safety is crucial: every home should have at least one smoke detector, complete with a ten-year battery. If there isn't one in your parents' home, it's fairly simple to install one at nominal cost. However, any suggestion of installing any form of security device or alarm system should be low-key. Don't create panic by labouring the point of their vulnerability. Explain you believe it's a good idea to install a security or panic button as a precautionary measure.

If they live in a city, they're probably super-conscious of security. But burglaries and muggings aren't restricted to cities. If they demur because they're in a peaceful, rural spot, you could say you're willing to organise and pay for it if needed – because you think it's well worth the expense for everyone's peace of mind.

People on low incomes may be entitled to financial help with security costs via their local authority's social services department – but this depends on local policy and individual circumstances. Check with the local authority.

Installing a panic button

One really useful home-support security service, organised through the charity Help the Aged, is the HandyVan scheme. Trained HandyVan fitters are based in key areas around the UK. They will go to any home, give a free security check, estimate the cost and then, once the work is agreed, fit door chains, viewers, window locks and smoke detectors in the home of an elderly person.

Anyone who would prefer a more sophisticated form of security, i.e. a pendant alarm which, on being pressed, links them directly to a central call-response unit at any time, can contact Help the Aged's SeniorLink unit who will organise supply and delivery of this type of pendant alarm.

Bear in mind that this 'plug in and go' alarm can only be fitted to a modern telephone line; there must also be a 13 amp electric socket within 3.6m (12 ft) of the phone line.

Both the HandyVan security installation and the pendant alarm can be supplied free of charge to anyone over 60 who does not pay income tax, does not live in residential sheltered accommodation and has savings under £20,000 (not including the value of their home).

Outside these criteria, at the time of going to press, the cost of the pendant alarm is £209.39 inclusive of VAT and maintenance for three months. Maintenance charges are £24.91 per quarter.

When ordering the unit, you must provide contact details of two people who have access to your parents' home (i.e. neighbours or relatives nearby) for emergencies.

SeniorLink will also install another option, a door-alert button fixed next to the front door, and also linked to a response centre – a reassuring device for someone in an area with high crime rates. For further information, see Resources, page 232.

If strangers call

Your parents may have plenty of common sense anyway. But it doesn't hurt to run through a list of what to do if there's an unexpected caller.

SECURITY CHECKLIST

✔ Never let anyone into the home without a prearranged appointment or being sure of their identity, no matter what they may say. (Keep front and back doors locked securely at all times).

✔ If you're not sure of their identity, don't answer the door but ask the caller to return (on a fixed day, when someone else will be there, if possible).

✔ If the caller claims to be from a utility company or working for a meter-reading company but can't produce any identification, never let them in.

✔ All utility bills carry a clearly marked phone contact so it's relatively simple to ring and check if someone from the company has arranged to visit. Many utility providers also have a special safety scheme which older people can join. You could contact them, on your parents' behalf, to see what schemes are on offer.

✔ Do a spot check on window locks and sashes: if you have any concerns, get repairs organised sooner rather than later.

✔ If your parents are worried about persistent unwanted callers, contact their local police station. Check their local Neighbourhood Watch scheme (see Resources, page 233).

WAYS TO BOOST INDEPENDENCE

- Focus on the positive. It's much more helpful to focus on the things your parents can still do, rather than what they can't do any more.

- Don't underestimate routine. If your parents are sticklers for eating meals at fixed times or carrying out certain chores at certain times, encourage them to maintain these routines. A daily rhythm of regular mealtimes, activities and sleep patterns can actually contribute to longevity.

- Focus on hobbies: whatever they enjoy doing, even sedentary pursuits like reading or crossword puzzles, get involved yourself to encourage interest. Are your parents keen bargain hunters? Research local car boot sales – find them online or in local free newspapers – and offer to accompany them if you can.

- Make sure they still feel useful. As parents, they might not be able to help out physically any more – but they can still provide emotional support. Be very clear that you value their views and opinions when it comes to discussing your own life. You can't overburden them with your woes or be negative, but if you share the positive thoughts or events, they'll still feel involved – and needed.

4

Eating and nutrition

You really are what you eat. At any age. Yet most of us don't worry too much about our parents' eating habits until things start to go wrong with their health. However, even on a basic level, learning a little more on this subject can prove enormously valuable to everyone long before any problems arise. Because a healthy, balanced diet is a key factor in maintaining an active and independent life in later years.

Unless you're a diligent healthy eater yourself, you might not be aware of all the issues to do with food and older people. I certainly wasn't up to speed on all the major nutritional issues when I was trying to help my mother at home and regularly preparing meals for her.

When she first went into residential care, I eagerly studied the daily menu – and I was amazed. For there among the healthy soups, stews, salads, fruit and green vegetables I expected to see were listed fried dishes, red-meat dishes and daily egg alternatives – things I'd avoided serving Molly at home.

Eggs, I believed, were dangerous if not cooked properly – and you shouldn't eat more than one or two a week. Meat too, particularly red, wasn't a great idea: tough to chew and liable to block up a frail system. As for fried foods, weren't we all supposed to be steering clear of the Dreaded Enemy: Fat?

There was an element of truth in my thinking. A fatty diet can be hazardous. But I needed a nutritional update. Health experts did warn us to limit our intake of eggs (to a maximum of three a week) some time ago. But recently the Food Standards Agency removed the limit – a few eggs a week aren't likely to be harmful to anyone. They should be hard cooked (to avoid health risks like salmonella) but apart from that, eggs form part of a healthy balanced diet – for everyone. Yes, meat can be difficult for elderly teeth and most dieticians say too much saturated fat found in fatty meats isn't advisable. Fry-ups too should be an occasional treat rather than a daily occurrence.

What I didn't understand back then was this: a sensible daily menu for anyone, any age, is a menu offering nutrition, choice and a balanced diet. All good nutritionists will tell you, a little bit of everything won't kill you – provided you understand the words 'moderate amount'.

Damaging assumptions

Like many people, I believed that as we get older, we don't need to eat as much as we did before, the underlying assumption being that if a person gets to 80 or so, they've done well, so whatever amount they do eat that's fine.

Wrong. As you age, your dietary requirement for protein lowers slightly – but your need for important vitamins and minerals is roughly the same. So the quality of your daily diet actually needs to be better.

But what often happens is the opposite. Older people, especially those living alone, often slip into really bad eating habits without even realising it. Sometimes they forget to eat at all – though if you ask them, they might tell you they have, only because they've forgotten whether they did or not.

You may also get an all-too-common situation where an independent-minded but increasingly frail person living alone 'gets by' on snacks, i.e. sandwiches, cups of tea with biscuits – nearly all the time.

The consequence of this is inadequate nutrition, which can potentially cause many health problems. Good nutrition can actually help with or even prevent some complaints affecting older people, like sight problems, arthritis, diabetes, osteoporosis (where bones become thinner, leading to risk of fractures), heart disease and strokes. So the more we know about healthy food, the greater the benefit.

But while old habits might die hard when it comes to eating or preparing food, older people's eating habits can also change because of health-related conditions. Someone living alone with a painful physical complaint like arthritis, for instance, may gradually stop eating properly because trips to the kitchen and lifting and manoeuvring pots and pans are just too difficult to manage. And while there are many different types of specially adapted cooking utensils, cutlery and aids available to help people in this situation, families may not always be aware that a parent is struggling to eat properly. For further information, contact Homecraft Rolyan (see Resources, page 232).

What happens to our body

Our bodies alter as we age. For instance, the energy we require in terms of calorie load usually starts to decline from middle age onwards. And our muscle bulk (in both sexes) dictates our metabolic rate. Most older people's physical activity is less, so they're not expending as many calories (energy units) each day. So the less activity, the less muscle bulk. And that lowers energy or calorie requirement – by around 200 calories a day. Yet despite needing fewer calories, the daily diet still needs to provide sufficient vitamins and minerals – a case of quality rather than quantity, if you like.

In addition, taste buds also change, so we can tolerate much saltier food. One good reason why older people sometimes don't bother to eat very much is that food tastes too different, too bland. So they don't really want it. And because people do, over time, become pretty set in their eating habits, some people often end up eating more of the foods that they really like, such as cakes and sweets.

I knew little of this. And in the months before my mother moved to residential care, I would be shocked sometimes to see how hungrily she'd consume whatever I'd prepare when I arrived to make lunch three or four times a week. I knew a combination of arthritis and shaky mobility meant she'd stopped even moving around her flat very much. But clearly, when I wasn't around, even though Meals on Wheels were being delivered regularly, not much was being consumed.

Fortunately this situation caused no long-term problems. It certainly wasn't as bad as the cautionary tale (told to me by Rena, a care-home worker) of Mary, widowed and in her mid-eighties, who had recently moved to a care home.

A dangerous diet

'Mum doesn't eat much,' Mary's daughter Samantha told the staff there on the day she took Mary into the care home. 'She likes cups of tea and biscuits.'

Within 48 hours it was apparent to the staff that Mary could only manage tea and biscuits. But the tragic reality was this was not Mary's choice: she couldn't eat anything else because it was so long since she'd had a proper meal before her, she'd 'forgotten' how to eat with cutlery and digest an ordinary meal. She had to be taught all over again.

'It took us a couple of weeks to overcome it. She was quite undernourished but gradually we adjusted her intake and helped her to relearn how to eat a proper meal,' Rena told me. 'Now she eats everything we put in front of her.'

This problem, said Rena, was fairly typical of a situation in which a person lives alone, relatives don't visit very often and there is no input, for whatever reason, from elsewhere, e.g. local-authority social services.

'Families who don't see their relatives very much use phone calls to reassure them, and like many older people, Mary was telling her daughter she was OK,' recalls Rena. 'But most people don't understand how easy it is for older people to get trapped into quite dangerous eating habits, especially if they're living alone.'

Why you might need to motivate

You might worry about the food your parents get if they have to go to hospital. Much publicity has been given to poor hospital food – and the fact that some overstretched NHS staff simply don't have time to encourage a frail elderly person to eat very much – if at all.

This kind of 'awareness', however, creates a huge and incorrect assumption: that it is mostly in a hospital or care home setting that elderly nutrition is lacking. This is completely wrong. Most of this lack of awareness centres around what happens in the home. Concerned families might see a 'solution' to the 'will they eat properly?' problem in Meals on Wheels (see Chapter 6, Getting help, page 104) or even in purchasing a microwave for those still cooking for themselves. Which might help.

But the reality is, this may not always be enough. Enjoying food is a fundamental part of our well-being. So that encouragement to eat, especially if it's clear that someone is either unwilling or unable to prepare a cooked meal for themselves, does require consideration – and mostly, it is only input from relatives or friends that will make a real difference.

Why traditional eating habits can help

Many of our mothers spent much of their lives buying and preparing fresh food, purchased locally from small shops or markets. Anyone growing up since the early seventies, when food technology expanded and frozen or ready-made meals from supermarkets started to take precedence in British lives, has probably got a very different fast-food sensibility (although most older people have readily embraced the idea of supermarket shopping).

But if you believe your parents are stuck in the time warp of preparing traditional, mainly fresh meat-and-two-veg type dishes, that's advantageous. These might seem dull or unexciting to contemporary, more sophisticated palates but, in fact, such habits are far more likely to form part of a sensible, nutritional, healthy diet. (A recent survey of Second World War eating habits in Britain, when food was rationed and people had to be extremely frugal, revealed that while people may have been leaner, their overall diet – with limited sugar and fat, and plenty of fibre – was far healthier.)

So if they still shop and prepare their own food, such ingrained habits will stand them in good stead. But if you do get involved in preparing a lot of their meals, you'll know that healthy eating isn't complicated: you should easily be able to stick to their preferences and create meals that are tasty and nutritional, including a variety of different foods, mostly available in the supermarket. Remember, eating healthily isn't just about staying slim – it can also reduce the risk of heart disease, stroke, diabetes, osteoporosis and certain types of cancer.

What foods to include

Finally, here's a small list of top-ranking healthy foods and the diseases they can help prevent if eaten regularly and included in your parents' diet. It is by no means a definitive list, but these foods are all readily available in the supermarket.

HEALTHY EATING CHECKLIST

✔ Tomatoes, fresh or tinned (can help prevent arthritis and Alzheimer's; they contain powerful antioxidants).

✔ Olive oil (also helps prevent arthritis and Alzheimer's).

✔ Oily fish like mackerel, trout, salmon, pilchards, sardines and herring (all reduce the risk of heart attack because the oil contains fatty acids that decrease the likelihood of blood clots forming). Even if someone has already had a heart attack, eating oily fish twice a week can reduce the chance of another one. (Best choices: tinned fish in tomato sauce or olive oil.)

✔ Strawberries, blueberries and other soft berries (their antioxidants help support the immune system).

✔ Broccoli, cabbage, rocket and other greens (for important plant chemicals and folic acid).

Healthy eating plan

A healthy eating plan consists of regular meals, three times a day. These should include:

- Five portions* of fruit and vegetables daily (for essential vitamins and minerals)

*A single portion of fruit is one apple or a bowl of salad.
A single portion of vegetables is roughly three tablespoonfuls of peas.

- Plenty of carbohydrate foods, i.e. bread, rice, pasta, cereal, potatoes (for energy)
- Small amounts of dairy products like milk, cheese and low-fat yogurt (for calcium to help strengthen bones).
- Adequate amounts of protein, i.e. meat, fish, pulses, beans and nuts

Fruit and vegetables are rich sources of vitamins and fibre for roughage. People who eat plenty of fruit and vegetables are less likely to develop heart disease and certain types of cancer. Vegetables, in particular, can make a proven difference in protecting people's mental faculties. Recent research in the US followed 4,000 people over six years. Those who consumed at least two servings of veg a day had significantly better intellectual function than those who didn't: the equivalent of turning the clock back five years.

Remember too that frozen vegetables and fruit are just as good as fresh – the freezing process preserves their vitamins.

If your parents are already keen microwavers, there's no real problem with eating microwaved food, provided they don't consume ready-made meals with high salt or fat content. And cooked meals can be frozen and kept in the freezer, ensuring a continuous supply for fast microwaving.

What not to eat

Whatever the situation, if you think your parents' diet isn't healthy, don't ignore it and hope for the best: if possible try to steer them in the right direction. They may ignore your suggestions and carry on cooking whatever they like.

You can't really change this. However, you could have a bit more leeway if you are directly involved in their cooking or shopping. Either way, knowing what's best to avoid could prove beneficial in the long run.

Because it is widely accepted that a diet high in fat, salt and sugar increases the risk of health problems and makes people prone to being overweight, all snacks containing fat, added salt or sugar should really be kept to a minimum.

As for bread, while white bread is often regarded as 'unhealthy', white bread made with British flour is fortified with calcium, necessary in any diet at any age. So while it's advisable to choose high-fibre wholegrain or granary bread, a high-fibre white bread from the supermarket is an equally healthy alternative for someone who only likes white bread.

Are biscuits bad? The occasional biscuit, i.e. one with a cup of tea, once or twice a day, does no harm. Problems only start when biscuits are used as a substitute for proper food. But a lightly buttered slice of toast is much better than a biscuit for a quick snack.

Cut back on fat

But which type of fat is better?

Food containing saturated fats or processed foods containing hydrogenated fats should be kept to a minimum, to reduce the risk of heart disease. These fats are mainly found in pies and pastries, biscuits, cakes, hard margarines, processed meats, fatty meat and full-fat dairy products as well as palm and coconut oils. (Lean cuts of red meat or lower-fat mince are a healthier alternative for meat eaters.)

Monounsaturated fat, however, is believed to be beneficial to health. Olive oil, rapeseed oil and margarines made from monounsaturates are associated with lowering the risk of heart disease. So they are good for cooking.

Some amounts of polyunsaturated fat or fatty acids, found in vegetable oils and oily fish, can help lower blood cholesterol (high cholesterol increases the likelihood of heart disease and stroke). Monounsaturates remain the best choice.

Whoever does the cooking, these tips help everyone when it comes to eating less fat:

- Think of crisps or salty snacks, chocolate, biscuits, pastries and cakes as 'treats only'; choose low-fat versions where possible
- Grill or steam food rather than frying. If possible, limit fried food to just once or twice a week. Fry in a monounsaturated oil like olive oil or the cheaper rapeseed oil
- Opt for a low-fat spread. If butter is preferred, spread it thinly
- Serve smaller portions of roast potatoes or chips and, if possible, limit them to once or twice a week
- Use semi-skimmed or skimmed milk, not full fat
- Remove skin from chicken before eating

Cut back on salt

Too much salt is linked to high blood pressure, increasing the risk of heart disease and stroke.

If there is already a history of high blood pressure in your family, it is doubly important to avoid high salt consumption: the ideal consumption of salt is just 6 g a day.

The problem is that so much of the salt we consume is hidden in processed or certain tinned foods. While food labelling is now clearer on how much salt is contained in a product, it is usually 'amount of salt per portion' on the label, rather than the whole pack. Or the packaging lists the sodium, rather than the salt, content – and sodium actually contains a higher salt content.

A food product containing 1 g of sodium, for instance, contains the equivalent of over 2.5 g of salt. So whoever does the shopping needs to look very carefully at the labels.

Lower salt-consumption tips include:

- Not putting the salt cellar on the table
- Using more herbs and spices in cooking
- Avoiding salty snacks, e.g. crisps and salted nuts, savoury biscuits and some tinned soups
- Using half, rather than a whole, stock cube in cooking
- Steaming or microwaving vegetables rather than cooking in salted water (this helps to preserve vitamins too)

Cut back on sugar

Nearly everyone finds sweet, sugary food tempting. But it can be doubly tempting if you are housebound or inactive. As we've already said, the occasional ice cream, cake or biscuit is fine. But in the main, consuming excessive sugar in food and drinks should be avoided.

Some sugar-reducing tips include:

- Opt for sugar-free low-calorie soft drinks
- Use artificial sweeteners in hot drinks

- Use fruit, e.g. a banana, as a sweet substitute for biscuits or cakes

Eating problems

Eating can be trickier when you're older. Some people find it really difficult to chew or enjoy certain foods; older teeth, gums or dentures can create problems. And shakier or arthritic hands can find knife and fork handling awkward and certain foods difficult to cut.

Moreover, as people age, their concentration and co-ordination lapse – leading to spilled food and, at times, messy consumption. If you are around at mealtimes, you might want to suggest a napkin and, if you're frequently preparing the food yourself, use large plates with a scooped edge, which will help 'push' the food onto the cutlery.

The following ideas might help those with problems chewing or cutting up food:

Avoid:

- Salads (lettuce is especially difficult to cut up; chunks of cucumber and tomato can be tricky)
- Certain types of pasta, especially spaghetti (again; often too tricky to handle). Try pasta twists or penne
- All tough, chewy foods, e.g. dry roasts
- Cornflakes or bran (harder to swallow)

Eat or serve:

- All cooked, softer veg like carrots, cauliflower, broccoli, cabbage and mashed potato
- Casseroles or stews (softer, slow-cooked meats are easier to eat)

- Cereals like porridge or Weetabix
- Soups, especially those made with beans or pulses

Drinking

As we get older, we also lose the sensation of thirst. So older people can go much longer without drinking. We all need fluid to maintain body temperature and help flush toxins from the body, but older people need to drink frequently to keep body fluids in balance and prevent bladder infections. In elderly men, studies show that the risk of bladder cancer is reduced if they drink plenty of fluids.

Ideally, liquid consumption should be around 6–8 cups of fluid every day. Half of these can be tea or coffee (tea contains powerful antioxidants). The remainder should come from a variety of liquid sources, e.g. water, milk, soup or low-calorie squash (as these can provide an elderly person with additional nutrients). However, sugary or fizzy drinks should always be avoided.

Alcohol consumption also needs to be treated carefully. Alcohol and many types of medication interact badly. Even over-the-counter drugs, like aspirin or ibroprufen, can prove to be a gastric irritant when combined with alcohol – and can cause tiny stomach ulcers. And excessive alcohol intake can also result in falls around the home.

If you are concerned about your parents' drinking habits – again, a nightly glass of sherry or wine is fine, a bottle a night is definitely not – regardless of whether they are regularly taking certain types of medication, it might be a good idea to discourage them from drinking more than a small amount, or talk to their GP, if possible.

Remember, too, that we shrink as we age. Alcohol is therefore likely to have a stronger effect than it did in younger years. Because it's so widely available and is often seen as a bit of a 'lift', it's easy to overlook the fact that it can cause problems, especially if other drugs are being taken.

Suggested healthy-eating menus

Here are some ideas for meals that combine all the healthy-eating principles outlined above. Remember, breakfast is very important. Without it, there's an increased temptation to eat unhealthy snacks during the morning.

Breakfast

- High-fibre cereal with milk (to help prevent constipation)

or

- Wholegrain toast with Marmite (for Vitamin B). Use Olivio or an olive-oil spread with toast. Spreadable butters are also healthier because they are blended with healthy vegetable oil

- Cup of tea with milk, or fruit juice

Mid-morning

- A drink (could be a cup of tea) with a wholemeal digestive biscuit

Lunch

- 110 g (4 oz) of cooked meat (roughly the size of a deck of cards). This could be chicken breast, a small steak, a pork chop – or a piece of grilled fish

- Generous serving of vegetables, e.g. peas, beans, cabbage, cauliflower with boiled or roast potatoes or rice

or

- Pasta coils with ready-made tomato sauce (nutritional value is the same as home-made sauce). You can add flakes of tinned tuna to improve the protein content

or

- Microwave low-fat ready meal (of around 500 calories) with rice or vegetables

- Dessert: low-fat yoghurt, custard-based dessert, fruit-based mousse, rice pudding (this can be tinned) or fresh fruit (e.g. a banana or apple)

Snacks

- Rich fruit cake or light sponge cake is fine (any cake with fruit is a good idea)

Dinner

- Bowl of soup with beans, pulses or barley plus wholemeal bread. Tinned soup is fine provided it contains less than 1.5 g of salt (the equivalent of 0.6 g of sodium). Avoid packet soups, which have minimal nutritional value

- Dessert: fruit (grapes, bananas), plus low-fat yoghurt

What about the cost?

Food bills, especially if your parents are on a low income or are very frugal, should also be considered, but there are ways to maximise healthy eating while keeping costs down.

- Make casseroles and freeze them, rather than buying expensive meats like chops.
- When making a casserole, add extra protein in the form of red kidney beans or lentils and use less meat.
- Serve larger portions of bread, rice or pasta with smaller servings of meat or fish.
- Do not rely on ready-made meals or takeaways, particularly those high in salt and fat. They're not especially cheap.
- Buy UK-produced fruit and vegetables when in season. They're better value for money and less expensive than costly imported items.

Are supplements useful?

While it is widely believed that supplements are useful, taking a multivitamin tablet alone will not resolve the problem of a diet lacking the right balance of vitamins and minerals. Furthermore, supplements cannot provide essentials such as protein. Anyone who can't get out regularly or is housebound might benefit from a Vitamin D supplement, though it can be found in oily fish, and in small amounts in eggs and all margarines. Most of our Vitamin D comes not from food but from exposure to sunlight. So it's a good idea to encourage a relative to sit by an open window on a sunny spring or summer day if they can't get out and about.

Generally speaking, it is wise to discuss the idea of taking supplements with a GP or doctor before embarking on a course of any vitamin or mineral supplements.

In the kitchen

Finally, if your parents continue to cook, a spot check around their kitchen to see if there are any safety or practical issues you can tackle for them could prove valuable – and might prevent unnecessary accidents in the future.

KITCHEN SAFETY CHECKLIST

✔ Are the kitchen worktops easy to use and at the right height?

Are they struggling with an overhead grill or a grill pan for toasting? A simple pop-up toaster, costing around £20, could make life much easier

 Is the oven too low, meaning a lot of stooping and bending?

✔ Is the kitchen floor safe, i.e. non-slip and generally in good condition?

✔ Are there any trailing wires or flexes that could easily be tripped over?

✔ Have the gas appliances been safety checked recently?

5

Encouraging an active life

S taying active and occupied keeps us motivated. And being motivated means getting the best out of life. Yet many families worry that when their parents are faced with big changes – perhaps when health problems start to restrict their independence or following the loss of a partner – their motivation to engage with the world will shrink, leaving them unwilling to go out, develop new friendships and enjoy life.

This need not be the case. Unless your relatives live in real rural isolation they can, if they choose, get involved with many different kinds of social activities, entertainment or community options outside the home, whatever their circumstances.

They may be registered blind or unable to walk far. They may be comfortably off – or living on benefits. Yet if they're up for some form of social contact with others or want to pursue a favourite pastime or hobby, there's no real reason why they can't do so.

Having said that, the encouragement to take advantage of any of these options might well have to come from you. Older relatives, especially if newly widowed, can sometimes be nervous about a new environment, even more so if bereavement has resulted in a move away from a familiar area. They may feel under-confident about venturing into a new social situation, particularly if they're adjusting to physical changes that have limited their independence. Or, even if quite mobile, they might not be willing to leave their comfort zone, beyond an occasional foray to the nearest shops or visits to relatives.

You might hear quite a lot of 'It's not me to go to those places' or 'I'm not really up to it' if you suggest trying a local community centre, for instance. And you certainly can't push the issue too far. But in trying to help them see the benefits, i.e. outside stimulation, more company, a chance to explore an interest, you're not just giving them an opportunity to reduce their dependence on family – it could broaden their horizons. Going off, just once a week, to spend time in a different environment and to socialise builds up confidence and provides a sense of purpose – particularly after a lengthy bout in hospital or a bereavement.

First steps forward

Here are some tips for helping parents adjust to changed circumstances or a new environment:

- If they're recently bereaved, consider where they are in the grieving process. For instance, if their partner died unexpectedly, e.g. following a heart attack, socialising might not seem appropriate, as they may feel guilty at the idea of moving on so quickly.

- Try inviting them to stay with you for a while and then introduce the odd outing, like a concert or a visit to look at National Trust buildings, to kickstart their interest in life again.

- If their independence is now limited by frailty, don't underestimate the value of your company in the simplest terms. Even sitting out together in the garden for an hour or two on a warm sunny day can help them feel that life is worth living.

- Look carefully at local social options and introduce ideas gradually in conversation.

- Develop ideas slowly. If a parent tries out a social option once and seems unsure about repeating it, don't make a huge issue of it. They might just need more time to adjust.

- If you've been spending a lot of time with a parent, don't think you're relinquishing responsibility by encouraging them to socialise. See it as guiding them in a more positive direction.

- Don't push or cajole them into new neighbourly friendships. Outgoing people will find their social level quickly but shyer people need more time.

- If they're adjusting to reduced physical capability, be patient if they don't show much interest in socialising at first. Consider how it must feel to adapt to such changes; after all, you could be in the same situation one day.

- Don't dismiss everyday pursuits, no matter how mundane they seem, as 'a waste of time'. If Dad likes tinkering around in the garage for hours with no visible result, and it gives him pleasure, this is much more important in the long run.

Pets and vets

Enthusiasm for what life can offer starts in the home. If your parents are keen animal lovers, looking after a pet in later life can be a great motivator, giving a valuable sense of responsibility. Recent research shows that households with dogs tend to report fewer incidences of heart disease, mental illness or depression.

Like small children, pets keep people active: your mum or dad will leave the armchair 'to get the dog's tea', then make their own. And taking the dog out for a walk means important regular exercise. There is a level of emotional dependence involved in having a pet. And this is perfectly healthy, especially for someone accustomed to family life.

Pet welfare

These ideas might help older parents with domestic pets:
- If you've time, bulk shop for pet food yourself so there are good stocks at your parents' home.
- Vet's fees can be expensive. If a vet is needed, help by doing your own price check with a local vet and then comparing prices elsewhere.
- Eliminate worry about a big vet's bill by suggesting you put it on your credit card; parents can then repay you later.

- For non-drivers or those who can't get out easily, transport to and from the vet can be a problem. If you can't do it, suggest they use a local taxi firm (always remind them to book a taxi in advance for the return trip).

- If a parent is going into hospital for a week or two and family or neighbours can't 'adopt', check out the best kennels in the area. The cost won't be exorbitant for a two-week stay. Find local listings on the web or Yellow Pages.

- For advice or information on good kennels and catteries, a local pet shop is usually a valuable resource.

If a pet dies

Losing a beloved pet can be incredibly upsetting, especially when it becomes obvious that a sick or old pet needs to be put down. If parents accept this, always ask if they'd prefer to stay with their pet when it happens, though they may prefer just to leave it to you. Remember, there is a fee for this and for the pet cremation. (Home owners have the option to bury a pet in their garden, but those who rent usually find that landlords won't permit this.)

If a pet dies suddenly, don't belittle their loss: 'Oh, Mum, it's only the cat'; they might need sympathy and reassurance. And don't rush in with an immediate suggestion of a replacement either. See how things go for a couple of months. Then, if they insist they want another pet, help them find one. Generally, cats are much easier for those with limited mobility; dogs are better for the more active. Puppies and kittens can be too much work.

One useful option for finding a 'replacement' dog is to contact one of the RSPCA's rehoming centres, the Dogs Trust or Blue Cross, who sometimes have older dogs needing new homes. (An older dog won't need training and is more sedate.) Remember too that cats and main roads don't mix: a cat will probably be safer on a quiet estate.

Many older people worry about what might happen to a pet if they die. If they mention this, it will help them to know that you're happy to take the animal, if this is the case. Alternatively, contact animal welfare charities like the Cinnamon Trust, Dogs Trust or Cats Protection (see Resources, pages 233–4).

Getting out and about

Community associations

Where do you start if you think a parent might benefit from time spent outside their home? Your first suggestion could be the nearest community association. There are 1,000 community associations, village halls and community centres across the UK, providing a wide range of local entertainment and social activities for older people. Options include bingo, bowls, singing, exercise, dance classes, lunch clubs and, in some instances, computer classes. Inner-city groups of this type do tend to have bigger resources; in quieter, less populated areas, the activities are likely to be organised in a village hall or community outlet, run by a local church or faith organisation.

Cost wise, there are varying fixed charges for each activity. These are fairly nominal, i.e. £3–£5 per activity, and the subsidised lunches, costing as little as £2–£3, can be excellent value for money. Find the nearest community association on the web or at the local library. You could pay a brief visit yourself to check out the place before suggesting it.

Day-care centres

Day centres are another excellent social resource for older people with physical disabilities or mental health problems.

These are run mainly by local authorities, providing a cheerful, friendly environment and a wide range of activities, including games, music, gentle exercise and discussion groups as well as subsidised meals. Some centres offer extra facilities like hairdressing or chiropody. Here too there are nominal charges, based on affordability. Some day-care centres also provide prebooked transport to and from home.

Check for the nearest centre via your parents' local authority (on the website under adult social services department). Attendance is limited, however, to those fulfilling certain fixed criteria – and eligibility can only be evaluated after a social services day-care assessment (see Chapter 6, Getting help, page 96); in that sense, day-care centres are a key resource for those who need them most, so they might not suit everyone. But they certainly offer a regular break in a lively, supportive environment.

Voluntary organisations

Many, like Age Concern, organise activities or entertainments locally. In certain areas, there are lunch clubs, outings and learning activities such as computer training.

If you live some distance away from a widowed or divorced parent, you could suggest they try one of the special Sunday afternoon tea parties run by Contact the Elderly. This is an excellent small scheme, run by volunteers, specifically for over-80s living alone. Local groups organise once-monthly outings for around 10–12 people, who are invited to Sunday tea, hosted by a volunteer in the volunteer's own home. Transport to and from the host's home is also available. There are no fees or charges. The scheme is mainly concentrated in city areas in England, Scotland and Wales. For further information, see Resources, pages 235–6.

Voluntary work

For anyone who is used to a working environment and enjoys meeting people, some form of local voluntary work on a part-time basis can be a godsend if they're newly widowed or living alone. You only have to step inside a few local charity shops to see how valuable – and enjoyable – this kind of activity can be: ongoing social contact, a sense of feeling valued and a fixed date in the weekly calendar. Ask around in your parents' area or check websites of major charities like Help the Aged, Cancer Research or Age Concern; all operate charity shops UK-wide.

Other part-time options may include helping out in local hospitals or schools. Check out what is available at local libraries or the local-authority website.

Walking and exercise

The best things in life really are free. And the health benefits of walking for exercise are huge: a one-hour walk at a brisk pace five days a week can halve the risk of stroke and lowers the risk of heart disease in women. Even a half-hour walk each day improves stamina and strengthens bones and muscles.

Regular walking also reduces the risk of falling, helps control weight and enhances independence and well-being. It's also hugely beneficial to anyone who is depressed or anxious: research shows that regular walking can help lift the spirits.

Obviously, it helps if one or both parents have always enjoyed walking. But you could try encouraging an initially reluctant walker by offering to walk with them to a nearby park or beauty spot. And walking is not always a solitary pursuit: walking and gentle exercise classes are run by many local community associations or groups.

Other forms of exercise are equally beneficial. Swimming, tai chi or yoga classes, even climbing stairs or digging the garden regularly, help people remain fit and active. But before directly encouraging any form of physical activity, e.g. gym classes, do consider the parent you know, not the person you think they should be. If they've never shown any interest in exercise or outdoor pursuits, it just might not suit them. Focus then on more sedentary ideas or interests – and try to get them to walk with you whenever you get the opportunity.

For further information on local walking groups and exercise classes across the UK, contact the Ramblers' Association, Keep Fit Association and Countryside Agency – part of Natural England (see Resources, pages 236–7).

When walking is a problem

But not everyone is physically fit enough to enjoy regular walking or gym classes. And changes in mobility can happen quickly. You might find yourself suddenly pushing a previously active parent in a wheelchair after a fall or hospital stay. But whether it's temporary or permanent, don't view wheelchair use negatively – because a wheelchair means freedom for a housebound person, whether someone pushes it or they operate it themselves. It's really as simple as that.

Most care homes and NHS hospitals provide free use of wheelchairs on the premises. But in everyday life, however, there are part-funding options for disabled people on low incomes needing to buy manual wheelchairs. Check with your parents' local authority social services department to find out about eligibility.

The Red Cross may help with short-term loans of wheelchairs for up to three months, which can be useful if you plan to take a parent on holiday or if one is needed after a hospital stay.

However, if the situation is more permanent, or if someone can only walk very short distances with the help of a stick or walking frame (often the case following a hip replacement), it may be useful to buy a wheelchair to keep either in your car boot or at your relative's home.

Buying a wheelchair

Your local chemist may be able to point you in the direction of your nearest wheelchair retailer. You can also check on the web for a good supplier.

Prices for an everyday manual wheelchair start at around £1,000 and can go up to £2,000 for a more sophisticated model. A wheelchair is a Class 1 medical device, so should never be purchased online or direct from a catalogue. It must be tried out properly by the user.

Always check for an accredited supplier giving honest, helpful advice and efficient after-sales service. The most reliable belong to the British Healthcare Trades Association, which also provides useful leaflets and information on wheelchair use (see Resources, page 238).

Walking sticks

Many older people use a walking stick that isn't the right length, so they don't get the full benefit of it. The right size stick can help correct any misalignment of the body and encourage more frequent walking.

For further information on buying the right walking stick, contact Arthritis Care and The Walking Stick Shop (see Resources, page 238).

Giving up the car

When you've driven for most of your adult life, giving up means a huge loss of independence, especially if physical problems make it difficult to use public transport. In some areas with limited public transport, it isn't easy to get around without a car. So this decision is not easily reached. And if you suggest it, be prepared for some resistance.

Generally speaking, if a person is still able to drive safely and is confident on the road, there is no upper age limit for holding a driving licence. However, if serious health problems arise that might impair general driving performance, e.g. bad eyesight or poor co-ordination following a stroke, the Drivers' Medical Group at the Driver and Vehicle Licensing Agency should be informed; technically, the DVLA should be notified of any major change in a driver's health at any age.

Certain age-related diagnoses, e.g. dementia, do not necessarily mean giving up driving: the DVLA will contact a person's GP for medical reports and might ask for a driving assessment before reaching any decision. But anyone diagnosed with dementia is breaking the law if they do not tell the DVLA and could be fined up to £1,000. (Remember too that a dementia diagnosis means also informing the car insurance company, otherwise a policy may become invalid; for more on dementia, see Chapter 7, Key health issues, page 123.)

If you're convinced a parent should stop driving because it's no longer safe and they refuse to accept this, you (or any other family member or friend) can contact the DVLA by fax or letter, expressing your concerns, giving the person's name, address and date of birth. This is completely confidential.

If your parent ignores all communication from the DVLA, the authority has the right to cancel the licence. These are drastic steps; you might not want to take them. But it's useful to know about them. For further information, see Resources, page 239.

Taxis

If your parents really resist the idea of giving up the car, point out the positives of not driving. Here are some ideas, in addition to helping the environment:

- To get out and about, they can choose any local taxi firm they prefer and set up a regular account. (If you're involved in finding a firm, double check their reliability.)
- Giving up the car means no more car insurance, MOT or parking fees, let alone buying petrol. Jot down all the driving costs – and then show your relative a comparison with regular taxi fares. A vehicle is usually more costly.
- Not driving means less stress when finding your way around. Dad might point to his sat-nav. But they don't eliminate lengthy traffic tailbacks.

Flying

If everyone over 60 were to suddenly stop flying, airlines would lose a huge chunk of their revenue. Flying might be comparatively 'new' to someone born in the twenties or thirties, but in the last 40-odd years it has revolutionised the way people travel.

Generally, the question of whether someone should fly or not is health related. Airlines have no limits or restrictions on passenger age. And if one or both parents are nervous about flying, they've probably reached a consensus by now on how often they fly, if at all. But any health concerns should always be discussed with their GP before booking flights.

The most significant problem associated with flying is the risk of deep vein thrombosis (when a blood clot forms in one of the body's deep veins, usually the leg). Those at high risk for DVT blood clots are over-40s with a past or family history of DVT, and anyone who has had recent surgery, especially after hip or knee operations, HRT or cancer treatment. Obesity and immobility are two other key risk factors. There is some evidence that flights lasting three hours or more may increase the risk of DVTs if people remain immobile.

Anyone fitting any of these criteria who is worried about taking a flight should take their GP's advice before making any travel decisions, especially after surgery. Generally speaking, long flights should be avoided for three months after any type of surgery.

In-flight tips for lowering the risk of DVT include:

- Drinking plenty of water during the flight (this avoids the risk of dehydration)
- Avoiding excess alcohol
- Moving around the cabin during the flight every hour or so

Going places

Here are some ideas for planning holidays and taking your parents out:

- On family driving holidays, adjust your pace for much older relatives. On drives to France or Italy, for example, factor in decent overnight stays. If they insist: 'Oh, don't stop overnight because of us,' say you'll all benefit from the pit stop.

- Travelling any distance by train, coach or car can also involve long periods of immobility and the risk of DVT. Make sure everyone stretches their legs during motorway breaks or coach stops on longer journeys.

- If booking holiday accommodation with elderly parents, ask all the relevant questions about stairs, lifts, en suites and disabled facilities before paying deposits. If replies are vague or unsatisfactory, try another company.

- If you're not using a car, make sure you find out how close your holiday accommodation is to the main facilities. A nightly fifteen-minute stumble over unpaved roads without street lighting could ruin a holiday for a person who finds walking difficult.

- Watch out for those early morning flights. A 7 am take-off means checking in at 4 or 5 am – and then there's travelling time to the airport to add on. Getting up at 3 am to wait for a taxi can be hugely disruptive for a frail elderly person.

- If your parents are nervous about moving about in an airport, check all the airports' facilities for disabled support or help before booking.

- When taking a frail elderly parent out in your car, or even using a hire car/taxi service, take extra care helping them in and out of the vehicle. If you're unsure about doing this (or are physically restricted yourself), get someone to help, i.e. a friend or the taxi driver.
- When contacting restaurants to book family celebrations involving frailer relatives, always check wheelchair access and locations of loos beforehand. Climbing two or three flights of stairs might be problematical.
- Your parents might still be taking holidays abroad independently or with friends. But never rely on holiday companies to contact you in an emergency. Always make sure you have full details of where they are staying and, if possible, a hotel or resort contact number beforehand.
- If they're staying in a place without a phone, suggest they ring you the day after arrival or mid-holiday. Or encourage someone in the group to take a pay-as-you-go mobile phone with them, for emergencies.
- If parents won't fly, consider a one-day round trip by train with them to the Continent. It means a very early start – but it will brighten everyone's horizon.

Meet and mate

Yet another popular assumption about age is that once people reach a certain point, they lose interest in the opposite sex.

Nothing could be further from the truth. Both sexes, especially if widowed or without a partner, will enjoy and seek out each other's company if they're given the opportunity – irrespective of their age. Women tend to live longer than men: so a fit eightysomething widower who enjoys socialising may be more likely to find himself the object of female attention than a woman of similar age. Which isn't to say an older woman won't find male company in her own peer group – the real issue is whether she's keen to get out and socialise in the first place.

A friend's father, 93, died recently. He'd been happily living alone, shopping for and cooking his own meals, and taking four-mile walks daily, for over six years. For the last two years of his life he had a girlfriend, an attractive seventysomething. All this came after his second divorce – at age 87.

Maybe it would help if we stopped viewing old age as a barrier to change or even finding love again: if anything, within reason, it should be a licence to do whatever we choose!

'I hit the jackpot'

Phyllis and Arthur are both 93, and they live in sheltered accommodation in north London. They've been married for 12 years, a second marriage for both: they lost their respective partners over two decades ago.

'We knew each other quite well before we were widowed because we all came to live at the sheltered accommodation around the same time,' explains Phyllis. 'We weren't terribly friendly, just the odd cup of tea now and then as neighbours, that's all.'

But one day, as the pair sat in their communal lounge, playing cards with a group of residents, Arthur announced that he had to rush off to watch the 10 pm news.

'I realised I was a bit disappointed he was going home,' recalls Phyllis. 'The next day, I invited him up for a meal. Then we started seeing each other regularly. He'd just come to my flat, I'd make a meal and he'd go home like a good boy, no monkey business. We were never naughty: just good friends.'

This continued for 18 months. Until one day, out of the blue, Arthur proposed. 'He said: "Phyllis, I'm very fond of you. If I won the lottery, I'd marry you,"' recalls Phyllis.

'I said, "You'd be mad. We're 82. You've had a triple bypass, I've got arthritis and osteoporosis." Arthur shrugged. "We'll have our problems together," he smiled.'

Phyllis went home and rang her eldest son, Chas. 'He said: "Go for it, Mum". I said: "You're mad too. Anyway, he doesn't do the lottery."

'But the next morning, my other son, Derek, sent me a bouquet saying: "Congratulations, Mum". We were married a month later.'

Anyone meeting the pair can see they are perfectly suited – and blissfully happy.

'I'd say we were meant to be together,' says Arthur. 'We are quite similar, we look on the bright side of most things. People were astonished at first. But if a man's alone I don't see why he shouldn't marry – at any age. Really, I hit the jackpot.'

6

Getting help

You may now feel that the time has come to seek additional help for your parents beyond the everyday domestic help described earlier (see Chapter 3, Maintaining independence, page 39).

Perhaps it has become all too obvious that a parent is struggling with independent living: even simple tasks (like preparing food, going to the loo, washing or getting in and out of bed) are becoming frustratingly complex, because either their physical or mental well-being has deteriorated. And while you or your family want to help, distance or circumstances may mean this isn't possible on a regular basis.

You may know, through your earlier research, that a state-funded system, via local authorities, exists to help older people. You may also know relatives who have previously been helped at home in this way, usually by a home-care worker visiting them daily. And you may want to try to get this type of support for your parents. Be warned, however: this is the most complex of the practical issues involved in helping older people.

Why? There are two reasons. First, there is no uniform, one-size-fits-all policy when it comes to getting home-care support services. Because while the authorities are handed specific sums of money for this by the government, each local authority has a different amount of money to spend – and they each spend it in a different way.

You've probably heard about the UK's 'postcode lottery': the way NHS funding varies locally. This also applies when it comes to getting state-funded care services for elderly people.

Where your parents live, therefore, is a key factor when it comes to determining how much state-funded help they might receive, which could be an important consideration if your parents move to a new area (see Chapter 9, Moving, page 165).

And whatever you may have heard about people's experiences, the reality now is that thinly spread resources mean that, unless needs are quite high, it can be difficult to get much help at home. The numbers of people now receiving state-funded help at home have dropped by 30 per cent over the last decade. So the more independent and active people remain, the lower their chances of receiving much state support. The frailest and neediest take priority.

As for who pays for this help, unless your parents are on a very low income, nowadays it's a case of 'user pays'. Moreover, the cost of all healthcare, including help in the home, increases all the time – a problem all countries are facing. From your perspective, therefore, it is better to start off realistically.

As for fees for services, each local authority sets their own charges. As a benchmark, however, people should pay around £15–18 an hour across the UK for care charges but this is likely to increase. Legally, the charges should be 'reasonable' and 'not likely to put someone in financial difficulty' (see Charges for services, page 97).

Approaching the local authority

If you or your parents decide to seek help from their authority, you need to contact the social services department (in Scotland, the social work department; in Northern Ireland, the health and social services board).

Any relative, friend, GP or even neighbour is legally entitled to contact local social services for help for an older person, provided that person agrees. (If they reject the idea of any help, e.g. if their mental capacity is impaired, this will be taken into account).

The following tips will help you when you ring the local authority:

- Explain clearly why you are ringing – and what you are hoping to achieve. Establish yourself as a key contact point. Give all relevant information. (It might help to jot down the main discussion points beforehand.)
- Avoid ringing first thing on Monday morning or Friday afternoon – public sector workers can be hard to pin down. Social workers tend to be seriously overstretched, so you may have to be patient.
- Don't be daunted if you don't get an immediate response: you have a legal right to seek out services from the local authority. Under the NHS and Community Care Act of 1990, all social service departments must

take down the details provided – and subsequently decide whether they can provide a service for an older person. It is called 'assessment of need', the gateway to getting this kind of help.

- Remember, however, that the 'assessment of need' isn't automatically offered to everyone. The authority decides whether it's necessary on the basis of what you tell them. And any assessment carried out will be in a 'queue' system, according to the level of need.

- If you think your parents' needs are urgent, say so right at the start. In a real emergency, local authority help at home may be provided before a full assessment.

- In some areas, self-assessment for care needs is now being introduced by some authorities. Internet applications are also being encouraged in some places; something you could do on your parents' behalf.

- If the authority agrees to carry out an assessment, expect a wait. But if a local authority care programme (or package) is set up and agreed, always ring immediately and insist on a review if things suddenly change and more help is needed.

- Never give up at the first hurdle. If you feel dissatisfied with the response or feel the person has not dealt with your query properly, ring back and ask for a senior manager.

- If you do get through to a sympathetic person who sounds helpful, get their name and direct line number for future reference, even if they eventually pass you on elsewhere. Someone who knows their way around the system can save you considerable legwork.

'If I hadn't made that call . . .'

Marie is 60. Her mother, Mavis, 88, lived contentedly in the residential section of a large care home for three years. Yet over time, she lost the ability to walk or stand properly and needed extra help from staff. The home had a small nursing section in the same building and wanted to move Mavis there. But the local authority (who had paid Mavis's fees since she first went into the home) needed to assess her before authorising the move because they'd be paying the higher nursing-care fees.

'The local authority visited Mum at the home in May,' recalls Marie. 'But nothing happened after the assessment. The administrator at the home kept in touch with me – but kept saying they hadn't heard a word from the authority. So Mum stayed where she was.'

Six months passed. The home reforwarded all documents and paperwork. Then came a faxed response: the local authority wanted a doctor's report. The home's administrator sent it off immediately. Three weeks passed. Still nothing.

'In the end, I rang the local authority myself,' says Marie. 'I didn't want to – the home weren't at fault in any way – but by now it was getting difficult for staff to help Mum because she was so shaky on her feet. She needed to be in the other section where they had hoists to help lift people.

'I got a very pleasant woman who heard me out and agreed six months was a long time. It wasn't her remit yet she rang me back with the details of the person overseeing the case: the paperwork had been lost.'

A week later, the financial approval came through. 'Mum was moved without any problems. I often wonder how much longer we'd have waited if I hadn't made that call – and got such a helpful person at the other end.'

What happens if problems are complex?

If a parent has serious health or disability problems, a 'comprehensive assessment' should be co-ordinated by a social worker or care manager to take place in your parents' home. The authority may then also bring in other people like a GP or district nurse. An occupational therapist or physiotherapist might be involved too to recommend aids, adaptations or exercises at home.

Should you be there?

It helps if you or another close relative or friend is at the assessment for back-up. Your parents might insist they don't want this, which you can't do much about other than explain that an extra person will help everyone – they might remember something important, for instance.

Who does the assessment?

It could be a qualified social worker or, depending on location, a community care assessor with home care experience.

What does it entail?

The assessment should take 30 minutes to an hour and is an overview of someone's physical and mental condition, their medical history, their personal care (i.e. problems with continence, difficulties with mobility or hearing) and relationships with others. The home environment and the person's ability to get out and about are also assessed.

What about finances?

If social services agree they can provide a person with support services, only then are savings, income and the overall financial situation discussed. This means test is to decide how much people can afford to contribute.

What is a care plan?

After the assessment, if support at home is available, a written care plan should be provided, which sets out a person's care needs and the help they are already getting. (This care plan is also used if the authority feels a person would be best looked after in a care home; see Chapter 9, Moving, page 164).

The plan should also give details of who will supply the home care, with relevant contact details, and your parents have a legal right to a copy. If they don't get one, request it immediately. Any questions should, if possible, be raised at the assessment. If you feel certain issues remain unresolved, consider making a formal complaint: local authority social services have a formal complaints procedure ring or check their website for details. It is a lengthy, bureaucratic process but it can result in an investigation if the complaint is serious.

Charges for services

If someone needs health services, e.g. a visit from a district nurse, as part of their care plan, this is provided free of charge.

But charges for home-care visits or Meals on Wheels depend on a person's income.

Anyone with assets or savings (including their home) amounting to more than £23,250 in England and Northern Ireland (£22,000 in Wales, £22,750 in Scotland) is likely to be charged in full for Meals on Wheels, home care visits or, in certain instances, care-home fees (see Chapter 9, Moving, page 165). Anyone with savings of less than £14,250 in England and Northern Ireland (£22,000 in Wales and £14,000 in Scotland) will not be charged for these services.

Direct payments

The authority is legally obliged to offer direct payments to anyone needing care, who is then given the money to buy it themselves. That way, they can make their own decisions about how their care is delivered – and who does it. These direct payments are not taxed and they do not affect any benefits received.

However, local authorities do not always mention direct payments if they agree to offer support; you or your parent may have to request them. Sometimes the local authority will refuse if they feel a person is not able to manage the payments themselves.

What other financial help is available?

Most state benefits for older or disabled people are means tested. However, the following benefits are not means tested and also tax free:

Attendance Allowance

Anyone over 65 can claim for this, regardless of their income or savings, if they need personal care with bodily functions, i.e. help with washing and dressing. They must be able to show that they have needed this help for the past six months or are terminally ill. For further information, contact the Department for Work and Pensions (see Resources, page 239).

Registered Nursing Care Contribution

This is an NHS-funded benefit paid to anyone receiving care in a nursing home (see Chapter 9, Moving, page 164). It is paid by the local primary care trust direct to the nursing home, who then offset it against the cost of care, depending on how much nursing care is needed. Current amounts are £108.70–149.60 a week in England. In Wales a flat rate of £119.66 a week is paid; in Northern Ireland a flat rate of £100 a week is paid in Scotland the flat rate is £69 per week. For further information, contact the Department of Health (see Resources, page 239).

Winter fuel payment

Currently set at £200 per household for those aged 60–79 and £300 per household for over-eighties. Anyone who pays their own care-home fees is still entitled to receive half their winter fuel entitlement. Those receiving full funding from a local authority for care-home fees do not receive any winter fuel payment. For further information, contact The Pension Service's Winter Fuel Payment helpline (see Resources, page 239).

Disability Living Allowance (DLA)

This is similar to the Attendance Allowance. It is for under-65s and has two components: a care component (for those who are sick or disabled and needing care or watching over) and a mobility component (paid out if someone has problems with walking or is unable to go out alone). For further information, contact the Department for Work and Pensions (see Resources, page 239).

These benefits *are* means tested:

Pension Credit

This is split into two parts: Pension Guarantee Credit and Pension Savings Credit.

Pension Guarantee Credit is paid to over 60s with a weekly income below the minimum amount the government says you need to live on (currently £132.60 a week for a single person, £202.40 a week for a couple).

Pension Savings Credit was set up to reward over 65s with modest savings. Anyone with a weekly income, including savings, of over £98.40 a week (single person) or £157.25 a week (couple) may qualify for Pension Savings

Credit. The maximum they can receive is £20.52 a week (single person) or £27.09 a week (couple).

For further information, contact The Pension Service or their Benefit Enquiry Line (see Resources, page 239).

Housing Benefit and Council Tax Benefit

These are paid by the local authority or district council. Housing Benefit assists with rent payments; Council Tax Benefit reduces the amount of council tax paid. Anyone on a low income living in rented property with less than £16,000 in savings can claim Housing Benefit; for couples, only one person may apply and joint income and savings are considered.

For further information on both benefits, contact the local authority or the Department for Work and Pensions website for application forms (see Resources, page 239).

Social Fund

Over-sixties with a low income, savings of less than £2,000 and receiving Pension Credit, Housing Benefit or Council Tax Benefit may be eligible for a payment from the Social Fund, a government fund that provides loans and grants to cover expenses not normally covered by benefits, e.g. funeral costs (see Chapter 12, Endings, page 223). For further information, contact The Pension Service (see Resources, page 239).

Carer's Allowance

Currently, this is set at £53.90 a week, but anyone with income over £100 a week caring full time for a relative cannot claim for this benefit. For further information, contact the Department for Work and Pensions (see Resources, page 239).

'We just struggled on'

Madeline, 60, recently sold her home in central London to move closer to her mother, June, 90, now living alone in Hertfordshire. June's husband, Alex, 97, has been in a nursing home 18 months. He has severe dementia and now barely recognises his family.

Madeline and her brother, Charles, had lived abroad for most of their lives. They were never very close to their parents.

'Mum and I had quite a distant relationship, mainly because she was so dedicated to Dad – always had been,' says Madeline.

'So even when Dad's memory started to go a few years ago and he started struggling with quite everyday things, like doing things around the house, we thought she'd cope.'

Charles and his wife had moved to live in the same village, so they kept an eye on things on a daily basis.

But Alex got worse and their local GP confirmed he had severe dementia. But the family were determined not to ask for any outside help.

'Mum and Dad are quite well off, so we knew state funding wasn't an option,' explains Madeline. 'So we just struggled on. Dad got worse and more childlike and Mum was just exhausted – she couldn't leave him alone for a minute.'

Eventually the family agreed they had to try to get Alex into a nursing home.

'We knew they'd be paying the fees out of their capital. But all the homes we contacted – apart from one – asked if Dad had had "an assessment". They told us they couldn't consider taking him unless social services had assessed him. We didn't really know what they were talking about; we assumed they meant his financial situation.'

Finally the family got Alex into a home that didn't ask for a social services assessment. 'Later, I learned that the other homes weren't legally required to insist on an assessment, it just suited them better.

'Now, of course, we realise that middle-class people who struggle on are at a disadvantage when the crunch comes because they don't go near the system. Dad now gets an Attendance Allowance, which isn't means tested. Because the local authority aren't paying his care-home fees, he's entitled to it. We didn't even know about that until a friend's mother went into a care home and my friend told me about it.'

What will a home carer do?

If your parents do receive home care from the local authority, variations in the way authorities run their home-care services mean that in some parts of the country, the home care could be a fairly limited service – and changing light bulbs, feeding the cats, cleaning the house or taking your mother shopping, for instance, may not be part of the equation. But most local authority home-care workers assist with basic needs and personal care, like help with getting dressed, taking medication, getting in and out of bed (but not lifting them) and helping with bathing and personal hygiene. Although the local authority will organise and oversee the care, in most cases the work itself is contracted out to an external home-care agency.

How many visits will they receive?

The number of daily visits depends on how much care or help is needed. It might be twice a day, morning and evening. Someone with a serious physical disability needing a great deal of care could be allocated four separate visits a day.

Meals on Wheels

All local authorities have a legal obligation to provide some form of sustenance for older people who can't cook for themselves. Some authorities deliver one or two weeks' frozen supply at a time; others organise daily delivery; some use external companies to provide the service. Anyone living alone who cannot heat the food themselves is entitled to help from a care worker to heat food.

Charges vary, depending on the area. Anyone receiving both local-authority home care and Meals on Wheels will be charged for them on separate invoices.

Finding a home-care agency

Your parents may wish to hire their own care help at home without involving a local authority.

In some ways, this is more straightforward, but it might be useful to request a local authority assessment first: the authority's care plan will detail all your parents' needs. (If you don't do this, a private home-care agency will want to do their own assessment.) Expect to pay upwards of £16 an hour, more for night-time rates.

To find a suitable agency in your area, contact the industry trade body, the UK Homecare Association, or the Care Quality Commission (see Resources, page 240).

If you're hunting for an agency on your parents' behalf, contact at least three by phone. If you like the sound of an agency and can visit their office in person, do so. (If they refuse to meet with you, be warned: any employment agency that refuses a face-to-face meeting isn't interested in anything other than the bottom line.)

If you have misgivings or aren't sure about an agency, trust your instincts. A half-hearted individual running the office might mean similarly unprofessional staff, even if the company adheres to all the correct registration policies.

Dealing with the agency

There is a considerable demand for private home care and increased regulation has done much to improve agency efficiency. But recruiting people to work in home care is a major issue: the numbers of workers have dropped in recent years. Yet a good home-care worker visiting regularly can make a huge difference to your parents' lives. Discuss it carefully with them before making any decisions.

Once you've found a suitable agency, make it clear to the manager that you'll be keeping an eye on things. Give them full contact details for you or your siblings. Establishing yourself as a key contact is useful if there are problems.

Don't think that by 'going private' your parents will get a superior or different service: the services provided by a private home-care agency are similar to those provided by the local authority. (If private nursing is required at home, some agencies provide registered nurses on an hourly basis too, though this is more expensive than hiring a home-care worker.) But the advantage of dealing directly with an agency is there's no intermediary to deal with.

Always consider the following points before hiring a home-care agency for your parents:

- The agency should provide a written contract within a week of starting the service. Pricing must be clear. It should explain what is included in basic charges and what is extra. Invoicing is usually monthly.
- Your parents must be kept informed about all issues concerning their care; ask that you too are kept up to date with these issues, if necessary.
- The agency must produce written evidence of confidentiality procedures and clear written instructions covering the way staff help with medication.
- The agency should: respect clients' privacy, treat them with respect and support them in maintaining their

independence. They should also make sure that their clients are safe and secure in their home when working with them.

Agency staff should always:

- Knock or ring the bell and speak before entering your parents' home
- Keep written, signed agreements detailing who has keys to your parents' home – and appropriate action to take if keys are lost or stolen
- Maintain confidentiality of details of entry codes to the house or flat
- Follow set procedures if they can't get into the home for some reason or if there's an accident
- Carry an ID card with their photo, name, employer and agency contact details

Lifting

One very tightly regulated home-care issue is to do with lifting people, as lifting can cause injury to a home-care worker.

If lifting is involved, discuss it fully with the agency before agreeing to hire them to make sure their workers have the necessary equipment, e.g. a hoist, to help them lift safely. If the agency says they have a no-lifting policy, ask how you can obtain a hoist before finalising any arrangements. If they sound indifferent or unhelpful, go elsewhere.

Timesheets

After each visit, the person receiving the care must sign a timesheet. It might seem easier to get a parent to sign timesheets once weekly or in advance, but this is not a good idea: they could be charged for a service they didn't receive. You could also check all invoices sent directly to your parents. If you're not living nearby, you may be able to arrange for invoices to be sent to you for checking prior to payment. In this case, check each one carefully. If it conflicts with what you know, query it. Mistakes do occur. (It's a good idea to keep your own diary note of home-care visits if you can; this can be useful if timings or hours are disputed.)

What if the care isn't suitable?

Whether it's local authority home care or privately funded care, they – or you – should always make a formal complaint if you or your parents are unhappy.

Send your complaint to the social worker who is handling your parents' case, whose name should be written on the care plan. Or ring the local authority social services team.

If you feel very strongly, follow up the call with a letter, fax or email. If you don't want a particular home carer to visit again, say so – if asked why, explain the reasons.

Sometimes the version of events given by the home-care worker or their manager will vary from your parents'. And it's fair to say that a confused elderly person might be talking about things that didn't happen. But if they seem upset or worried about repeat visits from a particular worker, ask for someone else.

Don't be scared to make a fuss or believe that your parents are being awkward: they have the right to complain if they don't get the right service.

If your parents are paying for their home care direct from an agency, use its formal procedures to contact them if there are problems.

Keep all copies of correspondence for future reference. If you feel the response is unsatisfactory, talk to your parents about 'interviewing' an alternative agency. If they're confused or you can't discuss it properly with them, don't let reason override your instincts: if the person 'helping' seems to be creating problems, do whatever you can to change the situation. Don't fall into the trap of thinking that any help is better than no help at all. Many home carers do a magnificent job. But an inefficient or lazy one can diminish the quality of a frail person's life.

Should you become a full-time carer?

Two million people in the UK care full time for an elderly relative. If you are seriously considering stepping into the full-time carer role, consider the following before making any firm decisions:

- Can you still maintain some sort of working life? You might believe you'll be caring for a short period – but it could be many years. People with chronic medical conditions now survive much longer, thanks to modern medical techniques. But once you fall out of the job market, it may be difficult to get back in.

- Take full stock of your own situation before making any promises for permanent change. Don't say, 'Don't worry, Mum, you can come and live with us,' without really thinking through all the implications. Talk to others in a similar situation before you decide: caring is rewarding, but it's also tough on the carer.

- Don't let guilt lock you into full-time caring. Consider the alternatives first. If possible, ask your parent: 'What's your ideal situation?' If they really want you to look after them, only then should you discuss it with everyone else involved, i.e. the rest of the family, especially your own children. Only do it because you really want to, nothing more or less.

- If you already have caring responsibilities (e.g. a disabled husband or child), make sure social services are fully aware of your situation. As a full-time carer, you are entitled to a carer's assessment from the local authority to review your own needs.

- If you give up work and are eligible for Carer's Allowance (see page 102), the government will pay your National Insurance contributions as for a full-time carer. This could eventually affect your state pension entitlement. Double check this at the outset.

For further help, contact Carers UK, the association that campaigns for carers, or Counsel and Care, a charity and advisory service for people over 60 and their families, advising on all community-care issues involving older people. Their dedicated Advice Team help with queries on finding help at home, care-home fees or advice on negotiating the community-care system.

The Elderly Accommodation Counsel is also a good source of information and advice about care and housing needs for older people. For further information, see Resources, pages 241–2.

7

Key health issues

We all want to stay fit and healthy. And we want our loved ones to stay that way too. Yet we're bound to feel a twinge of concern when certain age-related health conditions, like arthritis or diabetes, start to affect our parents' well-being. Or perhaps we suddenly learn, with some apprehension, that Mum or Dad's GP has given them an appointment at the hospital – 'for tests'.

Our concern is perfectly natural, but sometimes we could be worrying too much – even if those tests do reveal a problem. Nowadays, many diseases of ageing, often fatal for previous generations, are now treatable, which is one good reason why we're all living longer. Improved drug treatments or procedures for more serious illnesses like heart disease and cancer, for example, are extending many lives. And more important medical breakthroughs are likely in the near future.

As a result, a lot of the emphasis in older people's healthcare is on prevention, i.e. following a healthy lifestyle with close attention to diet, exercise and mental well-being. But it will help you to know a certain amount about what sort of health problems your parents could encounter – and the things you need to look out for.

Contacting the GP

The GP is the 'gateway' to NHS healthcare and the surgery a source of information and advice.

NHS treatment is now increasingly community- rather than hospital-based. Many procedures and tests for certain illnesses are now carried out in the GP's surgery or a local health centre. And free testing is available for many age-related complaints, including diabetes, glaucoma and high blood pressure.

If you're not living nearby and have concerns about a parent's health, researching their local surgery may be useful, as is establishing yourself as a contact point with their GP.

If you want to do this, discuss it with your parents first. Explain why it may be helpful to be kept up to date on their health concerns. Then introduce yourself to the GP by phone, letter or email, giving full details of your contact numbers, especially if you wish to be contacted in an emergency. Most GPs welcome this contact for older patients.

If your parents complain or believe their GP isn't giving a good service, you could suggest they try switching to another surgery. However, in many areas it is now virtually impossible to get onto a new GP's list. Contact their local primary care trust for information.

Health and the Internet

If you want to research specific information concerning your parents' health problems or complaints, there's no shortage of medical information available online. But some health sites are more useful than others. Some appear to be offering information and advice when in fact they exist to sell a product.

The most useful sites are either those from major health charities or those produced by doctors. They include: BMJ Best Treatments, Patient UK, NHS Direct, and Dr Foster (see Resources, pages 242–3).

Why minor issues matter

Smaller, less serious health issues can turn into bigger problems if they are ignored. Here's a brief list of the key minor issues to watch out for.

Feet

The right footwear is crucial: 80 per cent of people, all ages, wear badly fitting shoes. Yet foot problems affect mobility and can sometimes lead to falls. Anything affecting balance, like bunions, corns or untrimmed or ingrown toenails should not be left untreated. Regular checks from a chiropodist or podiatrist may be available via the NHS. Check with the local GP's surgery or primary care trust. In some areas Age Concern offer over-60s a nail-cutting service at local day centres; volunteers may even visit at home. There is usually a nominal charge. For further information, see Resources, pages 243–4.

Sleep

A good night's sleep is essential for maintaining good health. As we age, sleeping patterns change; people may nap more in the daytime, deep sleep patterns diminish and some people frequently wake during the night. Some medication can also disrupt sleep.

These sleeping tips may help your parents:

DO:

- Limit daytime naps to 30 minutes
- Limit liquid intake 2–3 hours before bedtime, including caffeinated drinks like tea, coffee, chocolate and cola, and alcohol (alcohol sends you off to sleep but is more likely to keep you awake later)
- Drink a warm milky drink at bedtime
- Go to bed at the same time every night; get up at the same time each morning

DO NOT:

- Eat large meals late at night
- Sleep in a stuffy bedroom with closed windows – a cool, dark room is better for a good night's sleep
- Rely on sleeping pills – sleeping pills are fine for 1–2 weeks in a crisis, e.g. a bereavement, but long term they can be addictive. And they may prove dangerous if combined with other medication.

For further information contact the Sleep Council Insomnia Helpline (see Resources, page 244).

Medication

NHS prescriptions for medication are free of charge to anyone over 60. But remembering to take medication regularly can be problematical for an older person with poor memory. For someone with dementia, it can be even more difficult, especially if they need to take tablets for different conditions.

One helpful method – for those taking more than one type of pill and whose memory is still reasonably good – is to tick off the different types of pills on a calendar.

If memory is poor, get a multi-compartment box from a local chemist; these boxes are marked with the days of the week and times. The box is filled at the start of the week, and is a very useful visual reminder of when it's time to take the tablets – helpful too if someone is supervising the medication.

Here are some other medication tips:

- If someone has difficulty swallowing tablets, ask the chemist if a liquid version is available.
- Always wash pills down with water (to stop pills from sticking in the gullet).
- Some capsules can be opened and sprinkled on food; check with the pharmacist.
- Do a spot check on the different pill bottles at your parents' bedside: if you're concerned about any medication, find out-of-date bottles, or discover they are

taking more than four different medicines, contact their GP or seek advice from the local pharmacist. A medicines review may be needed.

- Never suggest using other people's prescribed medication.

Teeth

In the past old age meant losing most – or all – teeth. Today nearly half of over-85s in the UK can expect to retain some natural teeth.

In later life, regular dental care is crucial; tooth decay and mouth problems can lead to eating difficulties and malnutrition. And the effects of gum disease worsen with age.

If possible, dental check-ups should take place every 12 months. Teeth should be brushed twice a day, and brushes changed every two months. (Electric brushes are helpful for anyone finding it difficult to use a manual toothbrush effectively).

Anyone in a care home should still be able to receive visits from a dentist; arranging access to dental services is part of a care-home's duty. And a housebound person can receive a visit from their own dentist or the local community dental service. For further information, contact NHS Direct or your local HSS board in Northern Ireland (see Resources, page 244).

NHS-funded dental care is not easily obtainable. In some areas it is virtually impossible to find an NHS dentist, and help with NHS dental charges is restricted to those on low incomes. To apply, collect a form from the local dentist's receptionist or benefits office. For further information, contact Prescription Pricing Authority (PPA) Patient Services (see Resources, page 244).

If you need a private dentist for a relative, the British Dental Association website lists around 6,000 dentists throughout the UK (see Resources, page 244).

Eyes

Eye testing is free, once every two years, for over-60s. Over-70s are entitled to one free sight test each year. (Under-60s already partially sighted or diagnosed with diabetes or glaucoma are also entitled to free sight testing.) If your parents have a regular optician, keep details for future reference.

Eye testing includes checks for the most common age-related eye problems: glaucoma and cataracts.

Glaucoma is a condition in which the flow of fluid out of the eye is obstructed, causing increased pressure in the eye. This damages the optic nerve and the nerve fibres in the retina. Untreated glaucoma can lead to blindness. If identified early enough, treatment (eye drops or tablets) reduces fluid production and pressure in the eye. Laser treatment or surgery may be used in more severe cases.

A cataract is a clouding of the lens in the eye. This prevents light passing through the lens and reaching the back of the eye, interfering with vision. Untreated it can also lead to blindness. The older someone is, the greater the likelihood of cataracts. (Over 70 per cent of over-85s have a cataract affecting their sight.) Treatment to replace an affected lens is usually by day surgery.

For further information, contact the Royal National Institute of the Blind (see Resources, page 245).

Hearing

Hearing problems are common in old age. If you notice any recurring symptoms or hearing problems, like some-one not hearing the phone or the front-door bell, they should be checked by a GP. An extra phone point installed by your parent's bed can be useful.

Ears are very sensitive – they play a big part in our bal-ance too. A simple hearing test can be carried out in the GP's surgery – or result in a referral to the ENT (ear, nose and throat) department of a local hospital.

Symptoms to watch for are: deafness, tinnitus (a ringing or buzzing in the ear, fairly common after 60), vertigo or dizziness, loss of balance, ear pain or a discharge from the ear.

Some ear problems are fairly straightforward; for instance, wax blockages – the most common cause for not hearing properly – are easily treated with ear drops.

For obvious hearing loss, an audiogram is a painless test; the usual solution is a hearing aid, of which there are many types. NHS waiting lists for digital hearing aids may be long – several months in some areas.

For further information, contact the Royal National Institute for Deaf People (see Resources, page 245).

For further information on health-related costs, contact Adviceguide, the Citizens Advice Bureau online resource (see Resources, page 245).

Other age-related conditions

Arthritis

Arthritis is an inflammation of the joints in the body.

The most common forms are:

- Osteoarthritis, mostly affecting the knees, hips, feet and fingers. Women are more likely to have osteoarthritis, especially in their knees and hands. It tends to develop gradually over time when joints become stiff and painful to move. A quarter of all people over 60 have pain and disability from osteoarthritis.
- Rheumatoid arthritis is caused by swelling and tenderness inside the layer of tissue forming a protective capsule around a joint. This prevents the joint from working properly. The inflammation can also damage cartilage and bone. This type of arthritis can develop very rapidly; it is important to treat the inflammation quickly to prevent long-term damage.

Treatments for both types include physiotherapy, surgery, medication including pain-relieving medicines (analgesics) or anti-inflammatory drugs, usually prescribed if there is inflammation and pain. Severe rheumatoid arthritis may be treated with steroids (artificial versions of the body's natural hormones), though these can cause side-effects over the long term. There are many types of immunosuppressant drugs that help as an alternative to steroids.

Regular exercise is very important for anyone with arthritis; ideal activities include swimming and walking.

For further information, contact Arthritis Care (see Resources, page 245).

Alzheimer's disease

The most common – and distressing – form of dementia, Alzheimer's is a physical disease causing a progressive decline in a person's mental ability. The illness prevents certain brain cells from working normally: the real causes of Alzheimer's are not fully understood. It can take 10–15 years to develop.

Symptoms vary. It may start with someone becoming more forgetful and repeating themselves. Or they may become more irritable, easily upset or unable to make decisions. As the illness progresses, short-term memory may deteriorate. The person may become confused about time and place – or their personality may change. Gradually, they may find they cannot carry out even the most basic of tasks, like washing and dressing, and then become dependent on others.

There is no cure for Alzheimer's. Drug treatments may delay the progression of symptoms but as with any form of advanced dementia, round-the-clock specialist care in a dementia unit may eventually be needed, though most people can be helped at home.

For further information, contact the Alzheimer's Society or Carers UK, who provide support and advice for carers and families of people with Alzheimer's (see Resources, page 246).

Cancer

The body is made up of hundreds of different types of cell. They all behave differently. Cancer occurs when a tiny part of the cell's mechanism goes wrong.

Half of all cancers first appear in people of 70 or over. But while cancer remains a huge taboo, early diagnosis can frequently improve chances of a full recovery. And advances in research and new types of drugs are giving more people a better prognosis than a decade ago.

The most common cancers in older people are lung cancer (more prevalent in men), breast cancer in women, and bowel cancer.

Free NHS breast-cancer screening is offered to all women aged 50–70 every three years and then on demand. A free NHS bowel-cancer screening programme was recently introduced for everyone aged 60–69 (50–69 in Scotland) every two years.

If a parent tells you about any of the following, urge them to see their GP immediately:

- A lump or sore that does not heal
- A mole that changes in shape, size or colour
- Abnormal bleeding
- A persistent cough or hoarseness
- Changes in bowel habits
- Unexplained weight loss

Treatments may include surgery, chemotherapy or radiotherapy. Some treatments may be deemed too aggressive
for a very frail, elderly person. All treatment should be
explained clearly beforehand.

For further information, contact Macmillan Cancer
Support (see Resources, page 246).

Chest Infections

Chest infections can be caused by many things: conditions
such as asthma or emphysema, exacerbated by smoking,
make people more prone to chest infections – but generally
speaking, older people are more prone to chest infections
because their immune systems can be poor.

Chest infections are often caused by immobility. And
they can develop very quickly, sometimes within hours. If
you see any obvious signs of drowsiness or dramatic
changes in a poorly or housebound relative's condition,
even if there's no sign of a cough or fever, contact a GP
immediately.

Dementia

The word dementia describes a range of conditions that
cause the progressive loss of the mental ability to remember, learn, think and reason. Dementia can sometimes
cause a gradual loss of social skills; people may lose the
ability to understand time and place. They may not even

recognise close relatives. Or they might believe things are happening that are not. While it is more likely to occur over the age of 65, dementia is not inevitable in old age.

After Alzheimer's disease, the second most common type of dementia is vascular dementia, caused by damage to the blood vessels supplying the brain. Another type, called multi-infarct dementia, usually leaves some of the brain's abilities intact.

Other, less common, types of dementia include Dementia with Lewy Bodies (DLB), which like Alzheimer's is not fully understood – symptoms are similar to those of Alzheimer's and diagnosis is often difficult. Rarer types of dementia are caused by damage to specific parts of the brain, alcoholism or by certain types of head injury.

Not everyone is affected by dementia in the same way. But because it affects a person's overall behaviour it can be extremely distressing for everyone. Some people may experience a rapid decline in their mental ability, while others in the early stages may have slight forgetfulness, or occasional out-of-character behaviour.

In some areas, local authority social services provide day-care centres for people with mild to moderate dementia.

The most accurate diagnosis of dementia is via a CT brain scan. A series of cognitive tests should also be used to see which part of the brain is most affected. Treatment may include drugs, but, in some cases, drugs can exacerbate problems. The best option for anyone with severely advanced dementia is usually a care-home setting.

For further information, contact for dementia, which runs a specialist helpline with advice from Admiral Nurses (see Resources, page 246).

Depression

Older people are more likely to have mild depression than any other age group. This is because depression is often a side-effect of illnesses like heart or lung disease, stroke or dementia. And it can be triggered by bereavement or even retirement. Symptoms include lack of energy, poor concentration, irritability, sleeping problems, lack of appetite, even tearfulness. Sometimes a depressed person will be persistently tired with unexplained headaches or abdominal pains.

Depression in later life can often go unrecognised, especially if a person with other health and/or mobility problems lives alone, which can create feelings of isolation. If you spot symptoms of depression, don't hope for the best – do everything you can to encourage an appointment with the GP.

Treatment is usually medication or therapy, sometimes a combination of both. If NHS counselling is not readily available locally (there can be a wait of several months), try a local mental-health charity like MIND, which may be able to provide some local support. If affordable, try private therapy. For further information, contact the British Association for Counselling and Psychotherapy or the Depression Alliance (see Resources, page 247).

Diabetes

Diabetes occurs when there is too much glucose or sugar in the blood. The level of glucose in the blood is regulated by a hormone called insulin.

Type 1 diabetes usually affects people under 40. It develops when a person stops producing their own insulin.

Type 2 diabetes usually appears in older people. It develops when the body cannot use the insulin it produces properly or fails to produce enough insulin to control the level of glucose in the blood. It is more likely to develop if there's a family history of diabetes or if someone is overweight. Undiagnosed diabetes can lead to blindness or kidney disease as well as a risk of heart disease and strokes.

Symptoms (both types) include: constant thirst and dry mouth, needing to urinate more frequently, weight loss, tiredness and weakness, blurred vision, a tendency to minor infections, e.g. boils, cuts or bruises that are slow to heal, or tingling or numbness of hands or feet. Diagnosis is by urine test.

Type 2 diabetes treatment can be a combination of diet and tablets, to prevent blood sugar levels from going too high. Anyone with Type 2 diabetes should eat regular meals, with a wide variety of foods. Sugary foods, fatty foods and too much salt must all be avoided.

For further information, contact Diabetes UK (see Resources, page 248).

Falls

Poor balance, ill-fitting shoes, limited vision or medication side-effects creating dizziness can all cause falls. And bad falls can dent the confidence of the most active person – as well as causing sprains, strains and fractures in a bone.

Common fractures in older people are of the wrist and hip. Anyone with osteoporosis is at greater risk from fractures from even a minor fall.

Sometimes someone will have a minor fall at home, but say nothing about it. Whether recurrent or a one off, any kind of fall should be reported to the GP. There may be a medical reason or a need for a 'falls risk assessment' at a specialist falls clinic to uncover a hidden cause. Specific treatments may help, like physiotherapy or occupational therapy.

Try pinning the following tips in a central place, in the kitchen or hallway of your parents' home. It will also help to quietly emphasise that if they do fall, they should always tell their GP, even if they manage to get up unaided without any sign of injury.

If you fall at home:

- Try to stay calm. Get attention by banging on the floor or a wall if possible
- If you have a personal alarm, use it. Or call 999 if you can reach a phone
- If possible, use a piece of sturdy furniture to try to pull yourself up
- Try to keep warm, pull a coat or blanket over you if possible
- Keep arms and legs moving by tensing your muscles

Heart disease

Although the number of people dying from heart disease has fallen in the last decade, mainly due to a decline in smoking, heart disease continues to be the most dangerous of all complaints, with around 270,000 heart attacks in the UK each year.

Coronary heart disease is caused when the arteries that supply the tissues of the heart with blood stop working properly because there are problems with the supply of blood and oxygen. This is called ischaemic heart disease.

The main cause of coronary disease is blockages in the arteries due to a build-up of sticky cholesterol, old muscle cells and clumps of blood platelets. This is called atherosclerosis. When this happens, there's less space for blood to flow and the stickiness means the blood is more likely to clot. The build-up also prevents nutrients in the blood being delivered to the wall of the artery, making the wall less elastic, and contributing to raising blood pressure.

Blocked arteries can be cleared by surgery as well as angioplasty and coronary artery bypass.

Angina is caused by a narrowing of the arteries supplying oxygen around the heart, a kind of 'cramp' of the heart muscle caused by blocked coronary arteries.

Symptoms include anxiety, shortness of breath, chest pain or pain that comes on with exercise but is relieved by rest. (If rest does not relieve the pain, it could be a heart attack.) Pain may sometimes spread into one or both arms.

Treatments include drugs, sprays, patches or injections. A small daily dose of aspirin may also be prescribed to reduce the risk of heart attack.

Heart attack – also known as a coronary thrombosis or myocardial infarction, a heart attack is caused by a sudden blockage of the blood supply to the heart muscle.

Symptoms include a cramplike pain in the chest that is not relieved by rest. Pain may spread to the jaw, arms or through to the back. Other symptoms include shortness of breath, nausea, dizziness, sweating, ashen skin colour and a rapid, irregular pulse. An urgent 999 call for an ambulance is always the best course of action even if the person insists 'it might be indigestion'. Giving 300 mg of aspirin to chew slowly could help – but check first if they are on any medication or are allergic to aspirin. Treatment is by either drugs or surgery.

For further information contact the British Heart Foundation (see Resources, page 248).

Incontinence

Incontinence, the involuntary loss of urine from the bladder, is embarrassing, distressing and can have a huge impact on confidence. It is more common with age, more likely to happen to women, and often under-reported: many people are too ashamed to admit to it. Untreated it can create hygiene and health problems.

If you notice it, always report it to a relative's GP, even if the person won't discuss it. In some cases, the solution may be a straightforward course of medication for a few months.

Why does it happen? Bladder weakness is more common as we age, though it's not an inevitable part of ageing. It's not always easy to determine the cause. Sometimes it happens when people lose mobility or can't undo their clothing quickly enough. It can be caused by weakness in the muscles controlling the opening of the bladder, drugs (especially some blood-pressure drugs) or by a urinary tract infection. Or it may happen if the bladder doesn't empty completely, leaving a build-up which eventually overflows – a type of incontinence more common in men. Severe constipation can also cause incontinence because it places pressure on the bladder. And if someone is badly confused, say with severe dementia, this may result in incontinence.

Equally distressing is faecal incontinence – losing control of one's bowels. This is rarer and is usually caused by weakness, tears or lack of control of the anal sphincter.

Urinary incontinence can be treated with certain types of drugs that help improve the bladder's muscle tone. These can be effective – but they need to be taken for several months. Faecal incontinence is extremely difficult to live with. It may need specialist investigation.

After assessment by a GP or social-services team, anyone with incontinence should receive free supplies of traditional nappy-style incontinence pads from the NHS. However, in some areas these supplies may be limited, as are other types of NHS incontinence supplies, e.g. plastic protectors for beds.

If affordable, however, certain other types of incontinence pad are more discreet and easier to use. A type of knicker pad, worn under clothing like normal underwear, is highly effective – and gives the wearer dignity and confidence.

For further information, contact Tena and the Bladder and Bowel Foundation (see Resources, page 248).

Osteoporosis

Osteoporosis can occur in both sexes but is more common in older women. People at risk include smokers, heavy drinkers, the physically inactive or those with a family history of the illness.

Osteoporosis, or brittle bone disease, means 'porous bones', in which bones are fragile and prone to break. It's often undetected until the time of the first broken bone: broken wrists, hips and spinal bones are the most common fractures with osteoporosis. Diagnosis is by measuring bone-mineral density by scanning.

Treatment includes certain types of drugs. HRT (hormone replacement therapy) is effective but not always advisable in older women with a family history of breast cancer. Calcium and Vitamin D supplements are often prescribed to help prevent broken bones.

For further information, contact the National Osteoporosis Society (see Resources, page 249).

Prostate Cancer

Prostate cancer affects nearly 30,000 British men each year. It is more common in men over 50 and one of the most treatable of all cancers.

The prostate is a gland in the male reproductive system located below the bladder. Cancer can affect the way the prostate functions and make urinating more difficult or painful. It can also result in wanting to urinate more often, especially at night. Other symptoms include: lower back pain, difficulty in getting or keeping an erection, pain in the genitals, hips or pelvis, and blood in the urine.

Diagnosis is by blood test; treatment can be either injections every six months, or by medication or radiotherapy. In some cases, prostate-removal surgery is necessary.

For further information, contact Cancer Research UK (see Resources, page 249).

Stroke

A stroke happens when the blood supply to the brain is cut off. The two main types are ischaemic (where a blood clot blocks the artery and restricts blood flow to the brain) and haemorrhagic (where a weakened artery bursts, allowing blood to seep out of the artery wall, damaging the brain by pressing on it). High blood pressure, age and family history are known risk factors.

Symptoms include a severe headache, unsteadiness, numbness, weakness or paralysis, slurred speech, inability to smile, problems with swallowing, and a sudden or gradual loss of consciousness.

Strokes can be fatal. Anyone suspecting a stroke should ring 999 immediately. Drugs may be given in the case of a blood clot, after a scan to differentiate between a blood clot and a bleeding blood vessel. Recovery depends on how much of the brain is affected: permanent brain damage can lead to paralysis. In some cases, a full and rapid recovery follows a stroke, usually in the first six months, though recovery can take several years.

For further information, contact the Stroke Association (see Resources, page 249).

Urinary tract infection

A urinary tract infection (UTI) develops when part of the urinary system becomes infected, usually by bacteria entering the urinary system through the urethra. Sometimes the infection begins in the urethra and, if untreated, it will travel through the rest of the urinary tract, causing a dangerous infection of the kidneys. Diagnosis is by urine test. Most UTIs can be treated effectively with a course of antibiotics.

Women are more prone to this; the urethra is situated closer to the anus than it is for a man, making it easier for bacteria to reach the urethra. In older men, UTIs may develop if they have an enlarged prostate gland. But generally, poor hygiene after a bowel movement, i.e. not wiping properly, or a weakened immune system will cause UTIs in elderly people.

Symptoms to watch out for include a burning sensation while urinating, cloudy, bloody or bad-smelling urine, pain in the lower abdomen and mild fever. A person may also become confused and unsteady on their feet, increasing the risk of falls.

The following tips are useful in preventing UTIs:

- Good hygiene habits: wiping carefully from front to back after going to the toilet and washing the genital area every day
- Drinking lots of water to help cleanse the urinary tract

- Avoiding scented bubble baths: chemicals in these can cause irritation
- Going to the toilet as soon as there's a need to urinate

For further information, contact NHS Direct (see Resources, page 249).

8

Hospital

It may start with a phone call out of the blue. Your mum or dad has had a bad fall and been taken to hospital. They're OK. But they need surgery. Or tests have revealed another problem . . .

This is a fairly common scenario. And when older relatives go into hospital, especially in an emergency, it can sometimes mark the beginning of big changes in their life, including losing some of their independence and needing more of your support.

Even in a non-emergency situation, say when someone is having surgery to improve their quality of life – perhaps a knee operation – few of us approach the idea of hospital with pleasure. Hospitals are places where lives begin – or are saved – but they still represent other things we often shy away from: illness, death – and temporary loss of control of everyday life.

So finding ourselves facing up to the declining health of a parent in hospital is sometimes a double whammy: it confronts us with our own mortality – and it's a cogent reality check that a parent may not be as strong as we'd thought.

Our parents too may feel the same unease: 'You won't get me in one of those places' is an oft-repeated senior mantra, and why not? Consider the prospect of losing your independence, even briefly, if you're in your late eighties and determinedly struggling to retain some control over your life.

Handling the hospital issue

So there are a lot of emotions churning around under the surface for everyone in this situation. Add the pace of modern life – where we expect to receive an efficient, fast service for virtually everything, including healthcare – and it could be said that coping with an older parent's lengthy hospital stay may be almost as difficult as it is for the parent. Although stoicism, putting up with difficult situations and not complaining, was often part of everyday life for their generation.

Another reason it may be difficult for families is that it can be distressing to see a once lively person reduced to mute, total dependence on others. Sudden frailty is a shock when it comes out of the blue. And if your mum or dad is confused about their surroundings or barely coherent, it can be painful to witness.

The other problem some of us may have is that, even if you haven't been near a public hospital for years, you'll have heard about the negatives: bed shortages, staff shortages, overworked doctors and nurses, overcrowded wards, hospital infections, elderly people on trolleys for hours.

Those stories may upset us or make us fearful – but they're nothing like the whole picture.

Yes, the care and treatment people get from the NHS may depend on where they live. But each and every day of the year, many thousands of older people are successfully treated in our public hospitals – and return home with no ill effect whatsoever. You just don't hear very much about the success stories.

The following tips might prove useful for dealing with your concerns:

- Try to see your parent's admission in a positive light. Rather than just being fearful of what might happen, understand the situation as an important way of supporting your parent.

- At home, parents may not want – or need – you to be their 'voice'; in hospital, even temporarily, you may become their spokesperson, their link with the world outside.

- Don't view hospital staff as people who are there to 'sort it' while you remain a passive onlooker. As overworked as they can be, good, professional nursing teams encourage input and communication from families of older people – because only relatives may know the small but important details that help them do their job.

- Your parents may be able to make their wishes known in no uncertain terms from a hospital bed. But even then, you and your siblings' presence can still make a huge difference – and speed them on the way to recovery.

'I was terrified – Betty took it in her stride'

Betty, 82, is an east Londoner with a warm heart and a lively take on life. She is no stranger to heartbreak. Married at 18, she lost her first husband, Derek, during the Second World War. She remarried later – only to lose her second husband, William, in a road accident.

'I'd always admired Betty, she's such a plucky soul,' says her former daughter-in-law, Julie, 51, now divorced from Betty's only son, John. 'She struggled to bring John up alone and sacrificed so much, working three jobs as a cleaner to make ends meet. But I've never heard her complain.'

John remarried and moved to Holland. So Julie has increasingly kept an eye on Betty, visiting her almost daily, and generally being the caring daughter-in-law she was before the divorce.

Eighteen months ago, Betty had an unexpected heart attack and was rushed to hospital. That evening, a worried Julie turned up – to learn that Betty needed an urgent heart bypass operation.

'Betty was quite calm about it – "Well, dear, I've not used the National Health, now it's my turn to get my money's worth," she said. I was in a panic. You hear so much about the hospitals, how they ignore older people, how people wait months for any operation – yet here was Betty, having major heart surgery the next day.'

That night, Julie hardly slept. 'I kept thinking of her lying there, waiting for the operation. It was stupid, I know. But I couldn't bear to think of anything going wrong.'

Julie's fears were unnecessary. The operation went well; within weeks Betty was back at home, lively as ever.

'She kept saying how lovely the nurses and doctors were to her – and how lucky she was to have such a big operation. To be honest, I visited Betty nearly every day and I never saw the same nurse twice, let alone a doctor. I didn't think much of the ward she was in either, it all seemed a bit chaotic. But Betty's attitude, laughing and joking with everyone, probably helped.

'The other day she said to me: "Hospital was like going on holiday, I met so many people" and I saw it through her eyes: she was able to get on with it because she trusted those doctors and nurses to do the right thing by her. And they did.'

PRIVATE HEALTHCARE

- Your parents may have full private health insurance cover. Or they may, like an increasing number of people, choose to avoid regular insurance premiums and pay for surgery when necessary. This is mainly because of long NHS waiting lists – and partly because private health insurance premiums, particularly for older people, are expensive.

- However, one important point to remember, if a parent is either insured or considering paying for surgery in a private hospital, is that many small private hospitals do not have the emergency resources – and intensive care units – normally available in big NHS teaching hospitals. So if something does go wrong, it may mean a transfer to an NHS hospital.

- Paying for private healthcare is a fairly straightforward process. Major health insurers now have a very accessible 'self-pay' fixed-price system, whereby anyone contacting them can obtain an estimated, all-inclusive price for a specific type of surgery, book an outpatient private consultation (usually within two weeks of contacting them) with a consultant of their choice, and be assured that after the consultation, surgery can be organised within one or two weeks in a nominated hospital.

- A GP referral letter is needed before the initial private consultation can take place. So it is best either for your parents to ask the GP to recommend a private consultant – or for you to help your parents research and find an appropriate private consultant before requesting the referral. A private outpatient consultation will cost around £100–£200; surgery for a hip replacement operation in a private hospital (the most common type of private surgery for older people) can cost up to £8,700 in London (this includes a five-night private hospital stay).

- For further information on private medical treatment, consult the Private Healthcare UK website or contact BUPA, BMI Healthcare and Nuffield Hospitals (see Resources, pages 250–251).

Hospital appointments

You may need to accompany an older relative on an outpatient appointment.

If you can't go with them, in some cases their GP may liaise with a hospital's transport department to organise transport to and from the appointment; in the main, patients (or their carers) are asked by the hospital if they require transport when the appointment is made. Given the huge patient numbers involved, NHS hospital transport is notoriously slow.

Your parents' local authority, the Red Cross or Help the Aged may also be able to provide hospital transport.

Here are some useful tips for accompanying a parent:

- Double check dates. Don't rely on your mum or dad's assurances that the appointment is on such and such a date. Ask them to show you the letter confirming the appointment and note all contact details, in case it has to be cancelled.

- Make sure you know parking arrangements or charges in advance. Hospital parking fees can be high and car parks crowded. In cities, parking may be scarce. If the hospital is some distance away, plot your route carefully, especially if travelling at peak hours.

- For short distances, consider using a local taxi service: less stressful than sitting in traffic and worrying about parking.

- Find out beforehand if the hospital has an internal vehicle or buggy system to transport people around. Larger hospitals are bewildering to navigate if you don't know the layout, let alone if you're frail and elderly.

- If your relative uses a wheelchair, take it in the car boot. Not all hospitals have a ready supply of wheelchairs in reception.

- Aim to arrive ten minutes or so before the appointed time; it reduces stress.
- If your parent is nervous or doesn't like the idea of medical students examining them, tell staff beforehand.
- Don't rely on the hospital cafeteria: take bottled water and fruit with you to snack on while you wait.
- Be prepared for a long wait. Even after the appointment there may be further tests. Or prescriptions for collection from the pharmacy.
- Should you accompany a parent into the consultation itself? Only if they insist. In that case, alert staff beforehand.
- If possible, use the day as an excuse for an outing. Ending it by going to a nearby café for tea, or a favourite restaurant for a light meal, can make it all much more pleasant.
- If an appointment does have to be cancelled, do it immediately. Even if you're told, 'Ooh, I think I cancelled it,' double check discreetly: that cancellation gives someone else a chance to be fitted in.

Planned hospital stays

If you know in advance that a relative is going into hospital for an operation, the following tips may ease the experience:

- Pack: letter of admission, glasses, hearing aid and dentures, if used, plus nightwear, dressing gown, appropriate footwear, i.e. day shoes and slippers, as well as underwear and day clothes.
- Toilet bag should include: shampoo, toothbrush, toothpaste, soap, denture cleaner, small towel, face-cloth and

travel pack of paper tissues, as well as any other toiletries, e.g. disposable razors for shaving. Any regular medications should be included too.

- Items of jewellery, large amounts of cash or plastic credit/debit cards should not be taken into hospital. Nor should alcohol or non-prescribed medication (like painkillers), which could be dangerous if combined with prescribed medication. £10–£20 in notes and small change should be sufficient cash.

- Many hospitals have TV hiring facilities on site: most wards have one TV. Only battery-operated radios can be taken in (plus headphones). Check hospital policy on this beforehand.

- If your parent is a smoker, see if you can persuade them to stop at least a week before admission. (This reduces the possibility of developing a chest infection). Remind them that smoking is banned within hospitals, and if they want to smoke they will need to go outside, sometimes a specified distance away from the hospital buildings.

- Mobiles are not popular; they can interfere with monitoring equipment. Most hospitals have phones by the bed – but these can be expensive for both incoming and outgoing calls. There should also be public phones in the hospital, and wards should have a direct phone line for people ringing in. Get this number from staff when you first visit.

- If accompanying a relative at admission, hospital staff will confirm all their relevant details, including your own phone details as next of kin. If there are any special concerns, mention them at this time.

Here's some useful information about being in an NHS hospital:

Legal rights

Older people are often intimidated by hospitals and view them as places where they don't have any rights. This is not the case. Anyone going into hospital has a legal right to a 'reasonable standard of care and treatment'. As for medical notes, a person may request sight of them – but this is not a legal right: each hospital trust has their own policy on this.

NHS hospitals should provide respect for confidentiality, privacy, dignity and a clean, safe environment.

A patient is free to refuse any treatment or medication, provided they understand what the refusal will mean.

Resuscitation

In the event of sudden collapse or cardiac arrest, all patients will be resuscitated if possible – unless there is a valid medical reason not to. In such circumstances, doctors may ask a family for their opinion on resuscitation. But the decision – which is very much an on-the-spot one – is the doctors'.

Making a complaint

If at any stage your relative feels unhappy about their treatment and you wish to make a complaint on their behalf, your first step is to talk to the staff, usually the nursing sister in charge or ward manager.

In England, you can also contact the complaints manager at the Patient Advice and Liaison service (PALS) located in the hospital to provide help and advice to patients and families. For further information in Wales, contact their local community health council; in Northern Ireland, the local health and social services council; in Scotland, all complaints go to the local NHS Board.

If this does not resolve the matter, you should make a formal written complaint, including dates, times and names of staff involved, to the chief executive of the hospital trust involved.

Complaints should be lodged within six months after the events concerned. Keep all copies of correspondence. If you are not happy with the trust's response, your complaint will then be reinvestigated. If you are still not satisfied, contact the relevant external body: in England, the Care Quality Commission (for complaints about private or NHS treatment); in Wales, the Welsh Assembly; in Scotland, the Scottish Care Commission (for private healthcare only). As a last resort, contact the Healthcare Ombudsman in England, Scotland and Wales.

Another useful source of information is The Patients Association. For further information, see Resources, pages 251–2.

Cleanliness

Cleanliness standards within NHS hospitals have improved – but they still vary.

There is a risk of picking up an infection in hospital, and the frail and those with poor immune systems are more at risk. MRSA is a micro-organism that lives on many people's skin, outside hospital. A person with a healthy immune system can carry it without suffering any detrimental effects. It becomes a problem if it moves from the skin's surface and into the bloodstream. While not all patients are screened for hospital bugs such as MRSA, anyone going into hospital for major surgery, like a hip or knee operation or heart bypass, will be screened beforehand. They will then be given treatment before admission to reduce the amount of MRSA bacteria on their skin.

As a rule, when visiting anyone in hospital, make it a priority to wash your hands thoroughly as soon as you arrive and when you leave. Alcohol-based gels and paper hand towels should be widely available in hospital toilets and washrooms as well as by patients' beds. This helps to reduce the spread of MRSA and other bacteria.

Patients should make it known to staff if they are concerned that a doctor or nurse hasn't washed their hands before treating them. If a relative tells you staff are not washing their hands appropriately, or you feel basic hygiene has been ignored, talk to the ward sister immediately.

Food

One of the biggest problems is making sure people eat and drink enough in hospital. Sickness aside, the shock of finding themselves in unfamiliar surroundings can often lead to poor appetite or even refusal to eat. And mass catering has considerable drawbacks – though in some hospitals there may be a choice of menu and a simple alternative, e.g. an omelette, can be requested by patients or relatives.

People don't have to rely completely on hospital food, however. If someone who normally eats well is obviously unhappy about the food on offer, the family can bring food like sandwiches or even takeaways into hospital, provided the person is not on a special diet or nil-by-mouth regime. Check with staff first.

If you are especially concerned about a relative refusing food, talk to the ward sister. And make sure staff are monitoring their weight.

Keeping up appearances

A stay in hospital means that normal daily routines are overlooked. But one thing that can boost confidence is paying attention to personal appearance. Sitting around in pyjamas or dressing gown and slippers all day does nothing for anyone's self-esteem.

If a parent isn't bedridden but normally takes pride in their appearance, ask if they want to get dressed properly. If so, explain to staff that he or she wants to be helped to dress each day. If you visit and this hasn't happened, ask again until it happens regularly. You may have to bring in a few different outfits and take dirty clothes home for cleaning. But the simple fact of wearing their normal clothes can make a difference, even to the frailest person.

If you have an appearance-conscious mum or aunt, help her by bringing in some make-up. If she is too weak to do it herself, offer to apply it for her – and do her hair. A male relative may want to shave, maybe with your help. Some hospitals have a mobile hairdresser visiting regularly or a hairdresser on site. Check with staff for details.

Long-stay problems

Sometimes an older person might be in hospital for several weeks, and they may become so accustomed to being there, that the idea of going back to the outside world may be unwelcome – because they've become dependent on others and lost confidence in their own ability to cope.

This tends to happen more frequently with people who live alone. One way hospitals try to overcome this is by organising, via social services, a brief home visit of around two hours, accompanied by an occupational therapist to check for any adjustment difficulties.

But in the hospital itself, visiting family or friends can also encourage independence. For instance, if it's appropriate, you could suggest taking a relative outside the ward for an hour or so. If they can't walk unaided, ask staff to organise a wheelchair so you can take them down to the hospital canteen or, weather permitting, outside for a short period. To an anxious elderly person, it could be a small step towards rebuilding that all-important confidence.

Here are some suggestions for helping elderly relatives in hospital:

- Get involved as soon as you can. Introduce yourself to the ward sister at the first opportunity. The ward sister (sometimes known as senior sister, charge nurse, matron or ward manager) should have a good idea about your parent's condition and developments in their care.
- Find out when ward rounds take place, so that when there's an update on your relative's care you can get the latest information afterwards.
- If it's necessary, talk to the consultant, who is the specialist doctor with overall responsibility and the ultimate hospital decision maker. Most have secretaries: ring them to book a suitable time to talk to or meet the consultant.
- Share visiting times with other family members; having other close relatives or friends involved makes the experience easier for everyone concerned.
- Bring in routine, if possible. Older people tend to have set routines and find hospital unsettling. Even organising something as simple as bringing in their daily newspaper can remind them of their lives in the outside world.
- Don't expect round-the-clock results. Emergencies aside, NHS hospitals work on a Monday–Friday routine. Social workers, dieticians and occupational therapists may all be involved in your parent's welfare – but not at weekends.
- If possible, aim for afternoon visits when ward activity tends to slow down. Arriving at the same time every visit helps too, establishing you as part of the hospital routine.
- Maintain the right attitude with hospital staff. Never be too timid to ask questions, and remember, being aggressive or angry won't help anyone. Be polite, clear, firm – and make it obvious that you want to know more in order

to help the situation, rather than be critical of any staff shortcomings.

- If you can't visit, regular phone calls to the ward are your only resource: you should be able to talk directly to your relative. Get the names of the ward sister and their deputy and ring to explain that you need updates. Book an appropriate time for phoning them.

- If one parent is in hospital and the other at home, work out a realistic visiting timetable. If the parent at home insists on visiting every day, help them do this. It may mean booking taxis or getting other family members to ferry them around, but for many devoted couples, separation is distressing.

- Try to keep emotions in check. If things don't look good and you're under pressure to work full time and visit frequently, try to keep a calm perspective. By all means, discuss your feelings with your family or close friends at home. But being tearful or panicky on the ward won't help.

Hospital discharge

This can be unsettling sometimes. If a parent has been in hospital for major health problems, it may mean huge changes (see Chapter 9, Moving, page 155) or alterations to day-to-day living arrangements, such as a care worker or nurse coming into the home.

The consultant decides whether someone is ready for discharge. The hospital healthcare team and, in many cases, the local-authority social services department, also have to carry out an assessment of the situation to determine whether an older person can manage at home again.

This may be the first time social services have been involved with your parents. In an NHS hospital, it is the joint responsibility of social services and the hospital to ensure that the right post-hospital care arrangements are made so that an older person can be discharged safely. (Anyone who is already a full-time carer of an elderly relative is entitled to his or her own assessment at this point.)

The chances are your relative will be going home. But there are other options that may be suitable after discharge. Hospital teams, including social workers, should always discuss these with you and your parent beforehand – even if they are returning to their own home.

If you're short of time, check to see if you can discuss these options by phone. A written care plan of what will happen once they leave hospital, e.g. some help at home, should be given to the person carrying out the care.

After-hospital options may include:

- A period of rehabilitation in another setting, like a different hospital, another ward or a residential or nursing care home.

- Intermediate care, for up to six weeks. This can mean temporarily moving into a care home or having a number of other services provided at home by the local authority, like someone to help with personal care. (Both rehabilitation and intermediate care should be provided free of charge by the local authority.)

- Services, equipment or adaptations to your relative's home to help them live there independently (here, there may be costs, depending on local authority policy).

- A permanent move into a care home (see Chapter 9, Moving, page 164).

If your parent's health needs have become complex, intensive or unpredictable, requiring 24-hour care or supervision by a nurse, they may be entitled to something called NHS-Funded Continuing Care.

Many families with elderly relatives leaving hospital are not always aware of this option. However, the criteria for receiving NHS Continuing Care funding varies between individual NHS trusts. But anyone with a serious illness could, in theory, have all their treatment costs and long-term accommodation in a nursing home, residential care home, hospital, hospice, or even a nurse in their own home, paid for by the NHS.

If you believe your parent's condition makes them eligible, talk to the consultant or doctor responsible for their treatment. Request an assessment for this funding – before any firm discharge arrangements are made. But remember, this option is only for people with extremely serious health needs, e.g. people who can't hold a conversation, are doubly incontinent or are bedridden.

CHECKING OUT

Here's a checklist of what the hospital must organise before discharge:

✔ Detailed information about any medication needed, plus a sufficient supply for at least a few days. If help with taking medication is needed, this should be written into the care plan.

✔ All information on treatment and medication should be sent to your parent's GP.

✔ Names and contact numbers of the people organising the care services they may be getting at home, e.g. a home care worker or district nurse.

✔ Confirmation that the hospital will organise transport for their return home if family cannot collect them. (Unfortunately, insurance regulations mean you can't accompany them on hospital transport.)

CHECKING OUT – CHECKLIST FOR YOU

✔ If you or another family member plan to be there on the day of discharge, start asking staff from day one: when will they go home? Bed shortages mean that unless a patient is there for a considerable length of time, the hospital will be planning their discharge almost from the time they arrive.

✔ Make sure your parent has a set of keys to their home while in hospital. Frequently, when people living alone are rushed to hospital in an emergency, door keys get left behind. The hospital has to make sure they can get into their home again before discharge.

✔ If you or your relative feel the discharge date is too early, talk to the consultant or ward manager. If you're still not satisfied, consider making a formal complaint, as described on pages 144–5. If a social worker is involved, talk to them too.

✔ If you're considering permanently moving a parent into your own home after hospital, don't let the emotional upheaval of hospital prevent you from thinking it through properly. Caring permanently for a relative or parent is a huge decision (see Chapter 10, What about me?, page 182). It should only be made following a period of thought and discussion with parents and family.

✔ If you can accompany a parent home after a lengthy hospital stay, staying overnight in their home for a night or two is a good idea.

Not everyone leaving hospital needs local authority care. If you live some distance away and are concerned about a relative returning home from hospital, try the Red Cross (see Resources, page 253). They may be able to send in a voluntary worker to help. This care-in-the-home service after hospital is specifically to help people living alone without family or with a frail partner. The voluntary worker will provide emotional support and help with shopping, collecting prescriptions and preparing meals for up to six weeks after hospital. But they do not provide personal care, i.e. helping with washing and dressing.

9

Moving

At any time in life, moving is high on the list of
stressful situations. Remember the last time you
moved house – the upheaval about fitting everything in, the indecision about what to part with? Now
imagine the prospect of that if you're in later life, maybe
frail, possibly widowed and still grieving, scared of what
change will bring, nervous about the idea of different surroundings.

Persuading parents that they need to move is, for many
families, a difficult step. It may be obvious that some sort
of change is increasingly necessary. But fear or concern that
pushing parents too far or too hard will result in the wrong
decision often leaves families floundering, especially if
there's parental opposition to the idea of leaving a home
they've lived in for many years.

Of course you can't persuade anyone to leave their home
against their will. But where it gets really difficult is when
parents reject the idea of moving, but their needs and
health have suddenly changed to such an extent that
there's no other option. So the move becomes a forced one
– and everyone feels unhappy.

Tackling the topic

The only way to anticipate the upsetting scenario of the forced move – which often takes place following a period in hospital – is to get to grips with all the moving options long before it becomes an emergency.

Once you understand the options, you can then discuss them with your parents, so they can reach some sort of decision with your help. Families that do this successfully usually come out ahead: if your parents are clear on what they really want when it comes to moving, it's easier to proceed accordingly.

That's the ideal scenario. But human nature being what it is, some families find it hard to make much progress in this direction: either parents won't contemplate the idea of moving at all while things are good or they're 'managing', or families feel too constrained to address the topic head on and make valid suggestions. In a way, both parties are held back by fear of the unknown and upsetting the delicate balance between existing independence and individual frailty.

This kind of stalemate can seem to bring all discussion to a standstill, but like most tough propositions, a sensible, straightforward approach may eventually move things forward: time spent looking carefully at all the options available will, at least, help you feel more confident about making any suggestions. And if you do tackle the subject with your parents, presenting it in positive, upbeat terms can help create some leeway.

How to have an important conversation

Here are some tips to help you when having that all-important talk about moving:

- Avoid having the conversation over the phone – a face-to-face conversation on a tricky subject like this is always better.
- Choose a good time: perhaps over an afternoon cup of tea when things are quite relaxed.
- Think beforehand about how you'd like to be approached on the topic. Try not to dither or beat around the bush. It's better to be straightforward and clear.
- Make sure you've done your homework, which may include discussing options with siblings. Have some factual information with you, e.g. photographs or brochures.
- Make sure you listen properly to what parents have got to say.
- Try not to use negatives. Rather than saying: 'What will Dad do if you get really sick, Mum?' point out what they might stand to gain from a new environment where more help is at hand.
- Don't anticipate the outcome – or think you'll get an instant result. It may take some time for them to think about things. You may have to return to the conversation at another time.

Why your reassurance will matter

Talking it through will also emphasise that if they do opt to move, they won't be handling the changes alone. This reassurance is especially important when one partner is newly widowed. Sometimes there's a different kind of 'loss' when one parent's health deteriorates to the point where residential or nursing care is the only option, leaving the other parent at home. If this happens in your family, it needs sensitive handling.

The parent left at home often feels guilty, that they've somehow 'let the other person down', even though they've done everything they possibly can. You can help by being positive and suggesting that by 'allowing' the move to happen, he or she will still be helping, by ensuring their partner gets the best care available. And, of course, the parent who moves needs to know that family support is there throughout to help them adjust to a new environment.

You may worry that neither parent will 'adjust' to any move involving separation and that it will have a detrimental effect on their emotions and health, which is an understandable concern. But never ever underestimate the resilience of the human spirit: despite outward frailty or even after loss, those concerns can prove misplaced.

'We did it as a team'

Millie, 85, has two children, living hundreds of miles apart in Australia. Her son, Roger, 55, an ex-policeman, is divorced and retired in Sydney. His sister, Elaine, 50, lives a two-hour plane ride away in Brisbane with her family.

The whole family emigrated to Adelaide from the north of England in the sixties. Roger and Elaine left to live in different cities. So when Millie's husband, Dave, died after a heart attack, there was a huge logistical problem: should Millie move near Elaine? Or would she be better off nearer Roger? It meant selling the family home and heading off for the unknown in either city. Could she cope?

'Luckily we'd talked about it before Dad died,' says Roger. 'Mum really wanted to move – but although Elaine wanted her in Brisbane, Mum wasn't sure: they do clash. Then, when Dad died, Mum said she wanted to move nearer me. She knew we might find something affordable about an hour's drive from me. Elaine was fine; it means a shorter journey to visit Mum than before.'

Roger spent three months in Adelaide with Millie, overseeing the sale of the house and the move. 'Mum amazed me. She's so determined. Most people of her age would have been weepy or worried. But she knew if she threw herself into the move, it would be easier. And it was. It was real teamwork.'

The pair organised a firm to transport all Millie's possessions and furniture to storage in Sydney. 'Then I drove her, slowly, to Sydney. We treated the drive as a holiday.'

'My home is tiny so it meant giving Mum the bedroom while I slept on the couch. But we didn't have a single quarrel while we house-hunted. And after a few months, we found something she liked: a little house with a garden near the coast.'

Roger helped her move in. 'She found it a bit strange at first, not knowing anyone. But two years on, she's settled in and made friends locally.'

'Dad would never have moved. But Mum knew what she wanted. We all grieved for Dad. But Mum was determined to turn it all into a positive situation – for all of us.'

Checking out the moving options

So what are the different housing options available? If your
parents are still fit and active but aware that their existing
home might not be suitable in the years to come, they
might welcome the idea of downsizing to a smaller house
or flat for practical reasons alone. And if you or siblings are
keen to encourage them to move closer to you, this is an
ideal opportunity to get the ball rolling by offering to look
around and check prices with local estate agents or on the
Internet. If they are keen to downsize for economic reasons, regardless of location, this is best acted on now rather
than later. No one knows where house prices are heading –
but they could still go up.

Here's a list of the other housing options:

Sheltered housing

This is a group of self-contained flats or bungalows. People
have their own front door and each flat usually has an
alarm system, often a pull-cord system linked to a 24-hour
response service. Most are one- or two-bedroom flats.

A scheme manager or warden is responsible for the
upkeep of the buildings – but has no input into the care of
residents. There are usually communal facilities, like a garden, lounge, laundry room or guest flat.

Local authorities or the voluntary sector (charities, housing trusts or associations) run most of the UK's sheltered
housing. Most properties are rented; in some areas you can
buy.

Rents for local authority sheltered flats vary, depending on where you live. There may be vacancies – but the housing won't suit everyone; in the seventies, local councils built groups of sheltered bedsitting rooms, but nowadays people want more space.

Sheltered housing run by the voluntary sector tends to be better quality, often with the option to buy. Prices vary but the best buy-in schemes will sell at market value; there's a thriving resale market.

Sheltered housing can be good for someone newly bereaved and living independently. However, needs can change. Some people become 'trapped' in sheltered housing if their health deteriorates. The organisation ERoSH (Sheltered Housing) is a useful contact (see Resources, page 253).

Extra-care or very sheltered housing

This covers groups of flats or bungalows with communal facilities that may be rented or bought. People still live independently but there is the huge advantage of care support on hand round the clock. Care staff are available on site – if needed, for example, for help with personal care.

These flats may also be purpose built for older people, with kitchens with lower units for wheelchair users or walk-in showers. Newer schemes are being planned specifically to ease the problems of confusion that arise with dementia, with safe outdoor space so residents can wander outside without getting lost. In some schemes, meals are also provided on site.

Extra-care housing is ideal for a couple where one partner is quite frail and the other is still independent. However, these are a fairly new resource. There may be waiting lists.

People wanting to rent extra-care housing from local authorities or the voluntary sector will need to have their care needs assessed by the local authority (see Chapter 6, Getting help, page 93); those buying from a private company may not require this.

Extra-care charges for the support services make it a much more expensive option than sheltered housing. But this type of housing is viewed as the future trend for older people's care.

For advice, contact The Elderly Accommodation Counsel (see Resources, page 253) or contact the local authority housing section in your parents' area for more information on their schemes.

These organisations provide good quality sheltered and extra-care housing to rent or buy: The Hanover Housing Association, Anchor Trust (which also runs retirement villages like Denham Garden Village; see below), MHA Care Group, and BUPA Care Homes (see Resources, page 254).

Retirement villages

Long established in the USA, these are quite new in the UK. Good examples include:

- Hartrigg Oaks, York, run by the Joseph Rowntree Housing Trust
- Westbury Fields, Bristol, run by the St Monica Trust

- Ryfields, Warrington, near Liverpool, run by Arena Housing
- Denham Garden Village, Buckinghamshire, run by the Anchor Trust

Retirement villages offer bungalows, detached houses and two- or three-bedroom flats for sale or rent with good security and disabled facilities (reinforced stair walls to accommodate a stairlift, for instance) within a village-style development which may include an on-site GP surgery, post office, village shop as well as gym, health spa and café. Residential/nursing care may also be provided within the complex.

This is an expensive option. In the South of England, a three-bedroom house in a retirement village can cost £450,000 – which may be more than the cost of a similar house in the area but not located in a retirement village – plus monthly charges for round-the-clock care help and communal facilities. But demand is growing, as people choose to downsize from a large family home to a safer, easier-to-manage environment within a small, secure community.

Telecare or assistive technology schemes

These are housing schemes provided by housing associations or local authorities in which technology is used to help people remain independent in their own homes. This can be a pendant worn round the neck linked directly to a call centre. Or an alarm system that can monitor a person with dementia if, say, they get out of bed in the night: the alarm is triggered if they don't return within a set time.

Telecare can help maintain independence but it's not yet widely available. And, in most cases, there still needs to be a person at the other end of the technology to react to an emergency situation.

Residential or nursing care homes (long-term care)

These are run by private companies, voluntary organisations or charities linked to particular trades, professions or religions. Some are run by local authorities.

The difference between residential and nursing care homes is that while both provide living accommodation, all meals, and staff to supervise care, give medication and generally provide support, residential homes do not provide nursing care, only personal care, such as help with washing, dressing and going to the toilet.

Nursing homes, on the other hand, provide personal and nursing care round the clock for people who are very frail, bedridden or have a medical condition that means they need regular attention from a qualified nurse. Because care is more specialised, nursing homes are more expensive than residential care homes.

Nearly 500,000 people live in residential or nursing care homes in England and Wales. Places are often limited, though costs are high: £300–£1,000 a week or more, depending on needs and location.

Care-home charges are calculated on the amount of care needed. So anyone considering moving to a care home should be assessed by their local-authority social services department to evaluate the level of care (see Chapter 6 Getting help, page 93).

Who pays for a care home?

In theory, those whose total assets are below £23,250 in England and Northern Ireland (£22,000 in Wales and £22,750 in Scotland) needing personal care could be funded for residential care by their local authority. (In Scotland, all personal-care charges in residential and nursing homes are state subsidised and local-authority charges for personal care given in people's own homes have been abolished.)

In practice, however, even if someone does have assets below these thresholds, local authority funding for residential care may not be automatic if they are assessed as needing only personal care: in many areas of England, Northern Ireland and Wales, the funding priority is for people with a higher level of need, like nursing care.

The general rule is that people with assets exceeding the thresholds will have to contribute towards the cost when moving into a care home. So the market value of their home may be taken into account as capital. However, since the local authority's decision to use this capital as a means of paying for care-home fees is discretionary, it is not always the case that the family home will have to be sold to pay for care-home fees.

For instance, your parents' home is not regarded as capital if a partner or a relative is living there who is either incapacitated and receiving Attendance Allowance or

Disability Living Allowance, or is aged over 60. If there is still someone living there who is under 60 (and not incapacitated), the authority cannot ask them to leave – or insist the house be sold immediately. What they can do (under their discretionary right) is put a legal charge on the property, so that when the home is eventually sold, the authority will be reimbursed for care-home fees.

Moreover, if you or any other family member live in the home and have given up your own home to be a carer, the home is not regarded as capital.

Families should also be aware of these points:

- Whether residential or nursing care is self- or state funded, people have the right to choose which care home they prefer to live in. However, many local authorities ask families for a top-up if there is a shortfall between the authority's set contribution for care and the chosen care-home fees. This has created huge controversy – the authority should always be challenged by anyone who feels the top-up is unfair or unworkable.

- When a local authority agrees funding, the home of choice does not have to be in the immediate catchment area of the authority. However, if a local authority nominates a home and it is felt to be too far from friends and family, a relative's psychological and emotional needs should be taken into account; the chosen home must meet all assessed needs for the authority to be doing its job properly.

- Whoever pays, there is no guarantee that the chosen home will have an immediate vacancy. But if the authority is paying, it should find a suitable alternative home where there is a vacancy.

Care-home fees and family finance

No one gets a free ride with care-home fees. Everyone living in a residential or nursing home in the UK has to contribute in some way towards the cost of their care.

Even those who are entitled to full funding for state care still have to hand over their state pension, savings income, pension credits or any social security benefits they receive to the local authority to pay towards their care, even if they have savings of less than £14,250 in England and Northern Ireland (£14,000 in Scotland and £22,000 in Wales).

The sum of money they are then allowed to keep (called a personal expenses allowance) is currently £22.30 a week in England, Northern Ireland and Scotland, and £22.50 in Wales – an unfairly small sum to cover things like new clothes, toiletries, postage or phone bills, let alone the occasional Christmas or birthday gift for relatives.

How fee planning helps

Despite the high cost of care-home fees, people tend not to plan ahead for them. This can be a mistake. Given our ageing population, this is a financial issue that really can't be ignored by anyone. If it's possible to sit down with parents while they are still fit and willing to discuss these issues, it could reap benefits. Careful financial planning may mean the family home cannot be included in a local authority's means testing for care-home fees.

Most married couples have legal joint tenancy of the home they own. However, if they are legally tenants in common, the property is effectively split in two – which means that when it comes to the issue of selling the family home to pay for care-home fees for one parent, leaving the other spouse at home, the home is excluded from any means testing. And if parents are willing to leave their 'half' of the home to children after they die (see Chapter 11, Financial issues, page 205), then any half share of the home that belongs to a surviving spouse stands a good chance of not being included in local-authority asset calculations either.

If parents are happy to change to tenants in common, a solicitor can organise it, sever the existing tenancy and set up a new one. The original deeds will be required. If there's a mortgage on the home, the solicitor will need to contact the lender. The cost is around £250–£300.

Means testing for care-home funding includes looking at income, savings, assets and investments. Investment bonds with a small element of life assurance are not included in these calculations. Even if parents have invested heavily in this type of bond, these cannot be included.

Other possibilities for paying for care

The deferred payment scheme is one option. Effectively this is an interest-free loan from the local authority. People only qualify for this if their other assets, property aside, are below the thresholds set out on page 165. The authority will then fund care-home fees but can put a charge against the property, so that when the owners die, the authority gets their money back by selling the property.

Renting property out

Another possibility, if parents agree, is to rent out the family home. This may be more appropriate if someone is widowed and going into care, and it can work well in areas with high rental demand. But you or a sibling will have to find and manage tenants and maintain the property. There may be 'voids' too – periods when the property is empty.

For further information on care-home fees, contact Counsel and Care, Saga, and Help the Aged's Care Fees Advice service (see Resources, pages 255–6).

Choosing a care home

The advantages of residential or nursing care are that they provide all care, accommodation, meals and activities under one roof and, in some cases, where residential and nursing facilities are on the same site, there is no need to move if health needs change. Friends and family can visit, and additional on-site facilities can include hairdressing, physiotherapy, a library, garden, activities, entertainment and outings.

Yet no matter how good the facilities, the quality of the care given should always be a major consideration. In some cases, a smaller home with a friendly, more 'family' feel could be more suitable than the more clinical, hotel-like atmosphere of a bigger, more expensive home with many facilities.

All UK care homes are inspected regularly by the Commission for Social Care Inspection. The Registered

Nursing Home Association provides national information on nursing homes only with lists in each area, and the Elderly Accommodation Counsel runs a helpful website called HousingCare.org. For further information, see Resources, page 256.

CHECKLIST FOR DECIDING ON A CARE HOME

✔ Look at a number of different homes. When you see one that looks suitable, discuss it with your parents – and even suggest an outing to look it over.

✔ Always phone first to make an appointment to visit each home. Explain that you want to meet staff and inspect the rooms and facilities on offer.

✔ Check the location: is it a quiet environment or near a noisy main road? Are there amenities close by, like public transport, a park, shops, cafés? (These can turn visits into easy-access outings.)

✔ Check the general atmosphere. Do residents seem happy and cheerful? A positive, happy atmosphere is a good sign.

✔ What do the fees include? Are there many extras? Are fees increased annually? Are they affordable for the future?

✔ Are there enough staff on duty – and how qualified are they? Do they seem friendly and engaged with the residents?

✔ Is the home clean and well cared for? Is there a garden? Is there special equipment, like bath aids or hoists if needed?

✔ Are the rooms comfortable with pleasant views and en suite bathrooms? Can relatives bring their own possessions and some furniture, e.g. an armchair and TV?

✔ Is the food good? Is there a choice of daily menus? Can they cater for special diets? Ask to see a sample menu and check out the dining room at mealtimes – if staff are clearly encouraging or helping residents to eat, that's a good sign.

✔ Are there set times for getting up or going to bed? Can residents stay in their rooms as and when they wish?

✔ Is there a guest suite or room for visitors to stay overnight?

✔ Is it a close call between a not-so-nice home close to family and an obviously better place that means a longer journey for visitors? Remember, you won't be living there. And a better quality home will make a huge difference to a parent's life.

Visiting

A well-run care home welcomes regular visitors. Weekend visits may be your only option – but if you can take your parent out for an hour or two then, even better.

If you are able to share the visiting with other relatives, it means more for your parent to look forward to.

Phones

Talk to staff about organising a set time to phone regularly. Check if there are public phones in the building for residents' use before requesting the installation of a direct line in the room.

A direct line isn't always necessary if parents are mobile-savvy. And anyone with mobility problems or at risk of falls will spend most of their waking hours outside their room, so that staff can keep an eye on them.

If using a public phone to maintain contact, try to ring at set times and tell staff when you'll be ringing.

Settling in

It may well take quite some time before parents adjust to the move and you may hear 'I want to go home' more than once. Try to accept this rather than worrying and telling yourself: 'We've done the wrong thing.' If you can, factor in extra time to be there for them as they settle in; otherwise regular phone calls will help.

Introduce yourself to key staff and make any concerns known immediately. Make it clear that you're always contactable.

Don't think short term

Many families treat visiting care homes in the same way as they do hospital: something to be endured rather than enjoyed.

However, if the care is good and parents settle in, they'll probably be there for quite some time. So chat to residents and staff and familiarise yourself with the place. If there are activities or outings, get involved if possible. And talk to other families who visit regularly; it helps to share your concerns.

Making a complaint

If you want to complain, start by talking directly to the manager or proprietor of the home. If there's no progress and your parents are paying, they have the option to move if the problem is serious and you're concerned about their welfare.

If the local authority is paying, contact their social services department and make the complaint by phone – and in writing by letter and email. Send copies of the correspondence to the chief executive of the authority.

If this does not resolve the problem, contact, in England, the Care Quality Commission; in Wales, the Care and

Social Services Inspectorate Wales; and in Scotland, the Offices of the Care Commission (see Resources, page 257).

Moving to another part of the country

Perhaps your parents are still independent and considering a move to another part of the country, to be closer to you.

Your first instinct is probably to encourage this; you'd probably worry less if they were closer. But first consider the following:

- Do they have lots of friends and neighbourly support in their existing area? Don't underestimate the value of a good friendship network forged over time. Losing those links can be painful in later life.

- Is your area right for their needs? Does the local authority have a good reputation? Is council tax higher? Are the hospitals good? Will they be able to get around easily and safely if they aren't driving?

- Will the new home be suitable for them if they become less mobile? Would it easily accommodate a wheelchair or a motorised scooter? Would it be manageable for one partner if the other died?

- Is your own situation likely to change? How would they cope if they moved near you and then you had to move out of the area?

You can't predict every possible outcome. But making this kind of move requires careful judgement. Discuss all the issues thoroughly with your parents before making the decision.

Should they move in with you?

This is a tricky dilemma. It may initially seem the most sensible idea, especially with a newly widowed parent. Your parent may have other ideas. A lot depends on:

- Your home and how many people live there: is it suitable for an older person?
- A parent's level of independence
- The strength of your relationship – if you've always clashed, it's unlikely to change if they're living in your home, even in a separate granny flat
- Your ability to care for them if their independence falters. If you work full time, could you cope? Would you be happy with care workers coming into the home?

Think long and hard beforehand – and, again, talk it through with your parents. Some people make the decision to house – and subsequently care for full time – an elderly parent irrespective of obstacles because they believe it's the best option (see Chapter 10, What about me?, page 182). And some parents will resist the very idea of living with their children, no matter how frail or dependent they become.

Packing up

Wherever they're going, helping your parents pack and leave the old home is an emotionally testing time. When it comes to sorting through or discarding a lifetime's worth of possessions, with all the memories that may entail, there's a huge finality to it all, a signing off, if you like, especially when leaving a big house for a small flat or a care home. These tips should help:

- If your parents are still very active and it's a planned move, turn it into a shared experience, where family or friends can chip in. Plan carefully; work out who will be responsible for what – and when.

- Make parents' input a priority when it comes to sorting out possessions. There might be a lot of 'Oh, don't throw that out, I need it,' when you know it's useless, but this is not a time to disparage things they value.

- First discard or throw out the unwanted, then pack what is to be moved. You may have to be very tactful about what is eventually thrown out. Enlist the help of removal people, if necessary, to take away unwanted items.

- If it does mean neatly boxing up and labelling cherished things they'll never use again – do it with good grace. If there's storage space at your home, offer to keep boxes there.

- Whatever you do, don't allow the disposal of things to become an opportunity for less-than-sensitive neighbours to pick over your parents' possessions. Other people's greed over even the smallest things can sometimes be surprising – and may upset your parents.

- Before the move, acclimatise your parents to their new environment. Take them for a look around and show them the positives: new shops, a closer bus stop and station, new entertainment options.

- Accept that you can't wave a magic wand over all the moving issues and concerns; merely do whatever you can to limit the upheaval. It may be exhausting, if you are directly involved. But if the end result is a better quality of life for them, it's worth all the effort.

But what if they won't budge?

Sometimes moving is discussed, but it never actually happens.

You may be totally frustrated because your parents simply refuse to budge, no matter how obvious the need for change. Accept it for now. Keep any research. Retain a detailed note of all the useful names and contact numbers and discuss a game plan for an emergency contingency with the rest of the family. If you live some distance from your parents, decide with siblings who should be contacted first in the event of an emergency and make sure everyone involved has lists of GP numbers and mobile phone details.

Here are some tips for families who do not live close to a frail relative living alone:

- If your parent uses a mobile, get them to store under 'ICE' (In Case of Emergency) the name and number of a relative or friend on their mobile phone list. Then, if there is a 999 emergency, crews know who to ring.

- For frail people with life-threatening conditions, all emergency services staff know about the Lions Clubs' Message in a Bottle scheme, in which a person's medical and personal details are kept – in a special green and white bottle – in the fridge. If the emergency services are called out, they can quickly find the bottle and pass on vital medical information to other emergency personnel. The bottles are obtained, free of charge, in local chemists or doctors' surgeries (see Resources, page 257).

- MedicAlert, also run by Lions Clubs, is another useful emergency tool, in the form of a bracelet or necklet detailing the wearer's main medical conditions, their next of kin, a personal ID number and a 24-hour emergency number. There is a charge for the bracelet and an annual subscription to join (see Resources, page 257).

10

What about me?

You may now find yourself in a situation where you're spending more time helping your parents because their needs have changed – and they're less independent. Perhaps you're juggling full-time work and family with regular visits, cooking meals for them or organising shopping, with or without regular home-care help from outside. Or you're managing to share the support with a sibling, who is equally busy with work and family.

If you've been doing this for some time, you probably feel quite drained – and it's fair to say you've probably overlooked your own needs a great deal. You may also, in the midst of all the practical concerns, be finding that your own feelings about what is happening with your parents – and how you can cope – are starting to affect you. You may feel frazzled, nervous, upset, stressed or worried. And if you feel the burden of your parents' welfare has fallen on you and you alone, even though there are siblings around, you might feel any number of conflicting emotions, including resentment (see Chapter 2, Family relationships, page 20).

None of this is unusual. But whether you're in a kind of part-time caring situation or are actually living with a parent as their full-time carer, the first step towards dealing with those emotions is to help yourself – by setting aside a certain amount of time for you and you alone, without feeling bad or guilty about it. Otherwise you'll run yourself into the ground – and then you won't be able to help anyone.

Somehow, you have to make room for your own needs, a 'space' where you can relax, enjoy yourself or let yourself be pampered. Or even pamper yourself. This is imperative, especially if there's serious concern about your parents' health.

Looking after number one

Here are some ideas that you can use. Following some of them will help you relax and make it easier to manage emotionally:

- Make sure you book time off from work in advance for breaks, no matter how short. This isn't just something to look forward to – it gives you a greater sense of control over things.
- Eat and drink sensibly. When you're rushing around all the time, it's so easy to reach for comfort junk food like salty or sugary snacks for an instant lift. Or indulge in overuse of nicotine or alcohol, two 'pain relievers' that actually reduce your ability to cope, as they lower the body's resistance to infection.
- Get some form of regular exercise that you enjoy. It could be the gym, swimming, yoga, a tai chi class or walking, whichever is easiest to fit in regularly.

- Give yourself time for some traditional pampering. It could be a hairdo, an aromatherapy massage, a manicure. Even if these options aren't possible, just half an hour in a scented bath once or twice a week, with your mobile off and the bathroom door locked so you can switch off completely, will help.

- Get enough sleep. If you don't, your body will eventually turn round and say 'stop'.

- Try to do the things you love most of all – whether it's gardening, reading, music, watching movies or a dance class, time out for your own satisfaction should never be underestimated. It's not an indulgence to enjoy yourself, it's a necessity in this situation.

- Maintain some kind of social life. It's so easy to lose touch with friends, stop seeing workmates socially or never go out for dinner with a partner when your spare time is so absorbed by helping your parents. Even if you can only manage one or two social outings a month, it's a chance to unwind and step back from everything.

- Keep an eye on your own health and maintain routine optician and dental appointments, screening tests or GP checks for any specific problems.

Facing your own fears

One big emotional consequence of helping older parents, even if you live some distance away and can't see them often, is that their increasing frailty may bring you face to face for the first time with your own feelings about growing old.

This is incredibly uncomfortable for some people. It can be challenging to consider our own mortality and to see ourselves as old and weak in the future.

For instance, you might be dealing with a situation where a parent is constantly forgetting things, everything seems topsy-turvy and chaotic and in the midst of trying to help them, a voice in your head says: Is this what will happen to me? Will I be like this when I'm old? Or perhaps a parent suddenly becomes seriously ill with an acute illness and you start to think: Is this hereditary? Is this what I'm looking forward to?

These are normal feelings. Unlike our parents or grandparents who lived in a much tougher world where the harsh reality of two world wars left families dealing with loss, widowhood or premature death virtually unaided, today's generation are considerably 'softer'. Many people now reach midlife without ever having really confronted the harsher realities of life and death.

An inability or unwillingness to face the reality of growing old may not apply to you. But if your fears about it are really getting you down, discuss them with someone you trust. Airing these thoughts will help you recognise that you are far from alone. Life's natural cycle runs this way: there must be loss and pain as well as happiness and joy.

If you're caring full time

You may have recently decided to look after a parent yourself on a full-time basis in their – or your – home. Perhaps the alternative – a care home – is something that neither you nor your parents would ever contemplate; many people feel very strongly about this. But at the outset, as a 'new' full-time carer, it is wise to think about the realities of the situation; emotionally and physically, a full-time carer carries an extremely heavy load.

What caring really means

The word 'carer' has many connotations. People may assume, for instance, that it's another kind of 'job'. In reality, caring is familiar territory: you've probably been caring for people throughout your life – friends, partners and work colleagues as well as family. So the truth is, you know how to care without thinking about it.

But it's fair to say that there will be times in this situation when you feel more 'caring' than others. We all experience a natural ebb and flow of emotions: days when we can tackle whatever life throws at us, others when we feel less enthusiastic about everything. There may be times when you feel you don't have the emotional energy to deliver – it's just too hard. That too is perfectly normal. None of us is superhuman. So accept your limitations right from the start. You can't afford to beat yourself up over the impossible.

Recognising yourself as a carer can be the start of obtaining outside support: you won't be able to do it all yourself all of the time.

However, you may well be disappointed by the quality of outside help in your area. But, once you've accepted what is available or worked out what else may help, you can handle the situation more realistically.

Don't ignore the system

If you've stopped working in order to care for a parent, get social services involved straight away. Ask your GP to refer you on or contact the local authority direct. (In Scotland, contact social work departments; in Northern Ireland, health and social services trusts). As a carer, you're entitled to your own assessment of need, though you're not obliged to have it. However, in some circumstances, it is social services who may be able to provide replacement care to give you a break or be an emergency back-up. A good GP should also understand the difficulties of being a full-time carer and may be able to help with referring you to other services, like counselling, if necessary (see Chapter 6, Getting help, page 93).

Let family and friends help you

You may be disappointed at the lack of concern for a parent shown by other relatives or you may have been too reticent in letting everyone know that you've chosen to look after them yourself full time.

Whatever your situation, there are bound to be family, close friends or neighbours who are willing to help out, visit your home, allow you a few hours' break once a week, or complete some small tasks on your behalf, like shopping or cooking. Don't always wait for them to offer – you may be pleasantly surprised if you ask for their input.

Don't get trapped into thinking 'no one else can do it'. At some point, you have to let go and trust other people to take over, if only for a few days so you can recharge your batteries. There is a fine balance between taking on a role in which you put someone else's needs before your own most of the time – and being a person who becomes a martyr for a worthy cause.

Consider your own health

Research shows that long-term carers are more susceptible to depression, high blood pressure and heart disease, problems that are sometimes a direct result of stress. Never quite relaxing or switching off because you're caring for a frail or helpless person can have an insidious effect on your well-being. For instance, in a crisis or emergency we naturally produce the 'fight or flight' hormone, adrenaline. However, continuous production of adrenaline – if you're reacting to demanding caring situations – can actually damage your health. For some relaxing ideas, see Looking after number one, page 180.

Don't ignore the future

It may not seem possible right now, but there will eventually be a time when you are no longer caring. And because caring can be so all-consuming, many full-time carers find life extremely difficult when it does end. They may feel aimless, without purpose. Which is why it is so important to keep some part of your life going, whether it's work, an outside interest or even study.

One woman I know, who cared full time for her bedridden father for six years without a single break, told me the only way she could keep her brain functioning was to learn another language. So, with the aid of tapes and books – and her father – she taught herself Italian. She created a real positive out of a situation that some would view as life limiting or negative.

Why it's all worth it

We live in an upside-down world. High visibility and outrageous behaviour are sometimes rewarded by attention and a certain kind of fame. Criminals become celebrities; celebrities who turn criminal maintain high-profile careers. But the millions of people who look after or care for frail, disabled or elderly people (or children) on a full-time basis are rarely acclaimed or even heard of; quietly, almost invisibly, they carry out what may seem like a thankless task to many people.

The truth is, this may be a tough and demanding situation but it's not thankless. Many full-time carers say that, in the long run, caring for parents can carry high personal and emotional rewards. Here are some insights into why full-time caring can be rewarding:

- There is an immense satisfaction in knowing you're there for your parents when they need you in exactly the same way as they were once there for you.

- You're unlikely to feel remorse or regret if you are a carer. By spending this time helping older parents, you learn more about them – and yourself. And this can eventually create positive and permanent memories of the entire experience – and their lives.
- Time spent with parents in later life also helps us truly appreciate their wisdom and experience. And it can enrich our understanding of humanity itself.

'There was no question of me not doing it'

Pam is 58. She has two older brothers and still lives in the small family home in south London where she grew up. Her mother, Clara, died two years ago aged 92.

'Dad died in his sixties. Mum was fine until suddenly, at 83, she had a stroke and a brain haemorrhage. She was unconscious for a week: they said she'd never survive. But she did. She was very frail. But after a month she came home. But everything had changed. She needed a lot of help.'

At the time, Pam worked full time as an executive PA. Initially, she was able to work part time for a few years. 'But things got worse: by the time Mum was 86 she needed me there all the time.'

So after discussion with her brothers, Pam stopped working.

'They were always supportive: one lives close by and could drop in; the other lives in Manchester but came down every few months to stay for a week, to help me.'

For five years, Pam cared for her mother at home, washing her, taking her to the toilet, helping her into a stairlift so she could get downstairs. Eventually, Pam needed an electric hoist to lift her mother – technically a task for two, yet Pam did it alone.

Financially, it was tight. 'But we managed. I had Carer's Allowance, Mum had her pension and Attendance Allowance. I had savings too from my job. If you're at home all the time, you don't need a lot.'

Pam's life revolved completely around her mother's needs. 'She was always bright, never miserable. But I wouldn't go on holiday. She couldn't travel; I wouldn't leave her. But I never felt any resentment. Mum sacrificed so much for us as kids. OK, I was the youngest and a single woman. But her love for all of us was so strong, there was no question of me not doing it.'

Yet caring for five years without a break of more than a few hours took its toll. 'I'd often be up all night with Mum; she'd want to go to the loo every 15 minutes. So I was exhausted. I went years without a good night's sleep.

'One night I just collapsed in the bathroom. I came round and Mum was sitting there on the toilet, saying, "Are you OK?"'

The next day, Clara told her daughter: 'You've got to put me in a home, this is killing you.'

'At first I wouldn't listen. But she argued with me.'

'It's the only answer,' Clara insisted.

Fortunately, Pam found a care home within walking distance of the family home, so she could visit daily. 'She was there for a year. She never moaned or complained. But suddenly, she became much weaker. You could see she was worn out.

'In the end, she just slipped away. Her last words to me were: "I do love my daughter."'

Pam has now returned to work. She is adamant that it was not in any way a sacrifice to do what she did. 'Mum was totally

*devoted to her children. Whatever we did in return was nothing
compared to what she did for her children.*

 'You couldn't have wished for a better mother.'

The guilt trap

Whether you're caring full time or doing your best to help
parents at home, one of the most complicated emotions
you can experience is guilt.

Guilty feelings – of having done something wrong for
which we alone are responsible – turn up in all our lives,
all the time. Mostly, though, its low level: sudden, intermittent reminders of small 'crimes' against others, like
forgetting a birthday or returning a phone call – everyday pangs of guilt that are easily remedied. However,
when it comes to concern for loved ones, especially older
or frail parents, guilt can prove to be a serious hazard.
The frailer someone is, the greater your concern – and
the more pressure you may place on yourself to do the
right thing by them all the time. Which is a totally unre-
alistic view.

Giving up a fraction of your life, no matter how small, to
help those you love is fine; letting guilt for what you can't
– or didn't – do drag you down into unhappiness and
remorse is no way to live.

You may have considered caring full time for a parent
and decided against it, yet still feel dogged by guilt for your
decision – even though there were a hundred practical reasons against it. Or you may have chosen to be a full-time
carer for a parent – but feel really torn and guilty about not

giving the rest of your family more of your attention. Whatever the situation, the trouble with guilt is that once you're carrying it with you, it has a habit of seeping out into the rest of your life – and affecting everyone around you.

Often, without even realising it, our guilty feelings can transmute into other negative feelings like anger or resentment. Then these wend their way into our daily behaviour. Irritated, frustrated and irrational, we end up snapping at everyone. Guilt can easily turn a pleasant person into a bad-tempered worrier. Which won't help anyone.

Understanding the guilt trap

It may help to understand where all this comes from. Let's imagine that guilt is an emotional currency, like pounds or euros. You may feel you 'owe' your parents a great deal, that there's a big (emotional) 'debt' for their time and love for you as you grew up. The problem is, emotional debt isn't easy to service – because no one is actually standing there, demanding payment!

Yes, there are emotionally demanding parents who manipulate their offspring into believing they 'owe' them for virtually everything. But that's the exception, not the norm. In the main, our parents don't push us into feeling guilty when we try to help them: we do it ourselves. As with ordinary debt, we either overstretch ourselves and try to do far too much, becoming seriously emotionally 'overdrawn' in our attempts to balance our own, often considerable, needs and our need to help our parents, or we believe, often mistakenly, that we're doing too little – and still feel bad because we're not 'paying back' enough.

Add to that our family history, where our past, often youthful misdemeanours may still haunt us – selfish times when we were careless of our parents' feelings, like battling with them as teenagers (a low point in many parent–child relationships) – and you may create a real pot-pourri of guilt and self-recrimination to deal with.

Managing the guilt trap

If your guilty feelings are troubling you, here's a three-step approach that will help:

Step one: Be totally honest with yourself about your feelings regarding what's happening with your parents. Write down your innermost thoughts and concerns. Ask yourself: are you focusing entirely on the parent you're trying to help, but completely ignoring your own needs or welfare, e.g. feeling too guilty to take even a short holiday, even though you're caring full time?

Step two: Now ask yourself, what can I cope with? How can I manage this situation better? What can I do within reason to improve things? By acknowledging your feelings about this and squaring up to them honestly, you should gain more insight – and this could stop you torturing yourself about what you can't do.

If you're trying to help a parent partly because you feel mired in guilt about things that happened long ago, for instance, you could become even more resentful and angry and you won't cope well. But by facing such conflicting feelings about the past head on, you can start letting go of them – because you'll see more clearly how they're actually holding you back. In turn, this will help you focus more clearly on doing whatever you can do for your parents.

Step three: Now you know that it is possible to manage the situation better, work out what is needed on a practical level to support that particular plan or idea. If this involves other family members or your partner, be honest with them about what you expect from them. It's no use saying to your children: 'You really ought to go and see Grandma' and then getting angry because they think it's mainly your problem. Tell them Grandma might welcome their visit and how you'd welcome their support – and why.

But if they're not going to be supportive, do not be side-tracked by guilt's best buddy, resentment. What others can't or won't do isn't the issue. Conserve your energy for the real issue, which is helping your parents.

Coping strategies

Whatever your situation, consider these ideas to help you cope:

- Intellectually, try to take it day by day; a one-step-at-a-time approach will stop you from becoming over-whelmed with concern or worry for your parents.
- Don't scare yourself by imagining all the worst-case scenarios that might happen – and then discussing them with everyone. When you're concerned about the

health or well-being of an elderly person, you can deploy a lot of energy on things that never happen.

- If you're actively involved in helping on a regular basis, stop trying to make everything perfect. You might be trying to create order, for instance, around your parents' home, as a way of feeling in control of the situation. But you'd be better off accepting that this is a less-than-perfect situation in a less-than-perfect world.
- Caring for someone is often a case of simply getting on with it, while making use of what help is available and getting support wherever you can.
- Professional help is good. But common sense is often likely to be your best guide.
- Accept that you can only do what you can.
- Our parents may not have always got it right. We won't always get it right ourselves. But what counts, even if you're some distance away from them, is knowing you did whatever you could. And that they know this too.

Finally, don't forget to approach your local authority, Carers UK, the Carer's Allowance Unit, the Princess Royal Trust for Carers, and Crossroads Care for help (see Resources, pages 258–9).

11

Financial issues

Cash is king, runs the saying. Well, it used to be. But these days, the plastic card, the pin number and the computer chip seem to have taken over when it comes to our finances.

Yet this isn't a reality for some older people. We may take technology for granted, yet a much older generation have never known anything other than cash. When they worked, many were paid weekly – in notes. Bills were paid in cash. State pensions and benefits were also handed over, in cash, at post offices. Millions of people used only a simple post-office passbook account in which to keep all their money.

Then, over the last decade or so, came enormous changes: direct payments of state benefits into bank accounts, more use of chip-and-pin technology, widespread use of Internet or telephone banking and, more recently, post-office closures. So what was once fairly straightforward may now seem quite complicated for the 'cash only' generation who are uncertain about plastic cards and the electronic world.

This might not sound like your parents at all: they might have adjusted to technological changes some time ago. But if health problems, especially those involving memory, start to affect their day-to-day life, there can be difficulties with technology: even forgetting a pin number can be distressing.

Many older people aren't overfamiliar with debt either. So if they do run into money problems, they often don't know what to do – and they probably won't be willing to confide in their children.

Some may still treat cash with great reverence, especially if they're living alone. They may store it at home, for 'emergencies' or 'just in case I can't get out'. Or keep it in different envelopes to pay different bills. If they've always lived by 'managing', they're probably still trying to do just that. To us, with our easy acceptance of mortgages, overdrafts and minimum credit-card repayments, this may seem like a struggle. To them, hoarding cash may be the safest – and only – way to feel secure.

Why money matters are so complex

Where your parents stand in relation to their finances is something only you and your family will understand. But whether they're cash-only users, converts to technology, or rely on an accountant, they probably won't welcome any 'prying' into their finances.

If your parents don't live nearby, you may understand their attitude to money, but how certain are you that they're handling it easily on a daily basis? Their financial 'health' could well be another area for you or a sibling to consider if you believe problems are beginning to emerge.

Even those parents who have reluctantly acquired a bank account in recent years may prefer to use it only to pay for big bills, simply because they're not used to banks and withdrawing money via the counter. Trips to cash-points may be difficult, particularly if mobility is limited: they may rely heavily on a neighbour or relative to drive them – and may worry about being mugged if they use one alone.

Stepping in to help

Circumstances may have already involved you in helping your parents with their money management. For instance, a recently widowed parent will probably welcome your help, especially if they relied on the other partner to handle all money matters.

But it's equally likely that they're less than willing to get you involved. Families often hit a brick wall here. After all, their money is often viewed as a personal matter or represents the ultimate security. In their minds, it is an ongoing provision for those they care for most, i.e. their family. Offer to change how they deal with that, even by helping, and they could feel annoyed. Equally, they could feel worried that this significant aspect of their independence, a remaining vestige of control over their lives, will be wrested from them. So they dig their heels in.

Sadly, there is no easy way to step in to help with your parents' finances. You need to use your own judgement.

But if you're noticing general confusion and you're often being told 'I've lost my keys/glasses/prescription/bill', this should alert you to memory problems making money matters confusing. (Don't panic and assume the worst if you spot this. While memory loss can be a minor manifestation of dementia – one in five people over 80 will have some form of dementia – it doesn't always signal Alzheimer's or dementia in a serious form. It's often just part of the general ageing process.)

If any of the following experiences sound familiar, then it is probably time to try to get involved. Discuss and explain that you think it might be a good idea if you – or a sibling – handled the financial paperwork or the payment of bills, in order to make life a bit easier.

- Telephone conversations about 'stolen' money or possessions. This is all too common, though many families go along with it, often believing their parent to be telling the truth, especially if there is a stranger, like a home carer, coming into the home. The reality is, it's usually just confusion. Nothing has been stolen.

- Unpaid bills. If the phone is cut off, for instance, because a bill remains unpaid, this could indicate a problem. In this situation, you may have to contact the utility company yourself, explaining the situation and quickly organising payment.

- Repeated payments for the same bill. You may not spot this unless you see bank statements or cheque stubs, but if you do, it's another warning sign.

- Finding money or anything of value, like jewellery or ornaments, hidden in an unusual place. This may be the 'stolen' cash you've heard about. Hiding money is not uncommon, but, all too often, deteriorating memory will mean the hiding place is forgotten.

- Conversations in which a person may insist they paid for something or handed over money, when all the evidence is completely to the contrary.

Taking over

Situations like these can be distressing. But they may help you persuade a parent that you should become more directly involved with their finances. If you are frequently hearing that money is being 'stolen', or are having conversations about 'lost' or 'missing' cash, try not to argue, no matter how irrational it all seems, as doing so will only cause further distress. Instead, use the conversation as an opportunity to offer to help. Saying: 'What can we do about it?' could initiate a fruitful discussion.

If your parents agree to accept your help, it may initially be quite simple. For instance, if your parents normally pay for everything by cash, offer to do this for them. If they have a bank account and cheque book, another way to help would be to ask them to sign the cheques; you do the rest.

If they are willing to hand over all bills to you and are happy with this arrangement, this can be a fairly easy way of managing their financial situation, perhaps with a once-monthly cheque-signing and sorting session.

You would then be able to file bills and keep important contact numbers for banks, utilities or insurance companies. If they use a pin number at the local bank or cashpoint, establishing a regular lift to help them do this will, in part, give them a sense of maintaining some independence and financial control.

Pin numbers can be a problem. Strictly speaking, we're all supposed to remember them without writing them down or keeping the numbers anywhere near the card. Yet some older people can't do that; they need a visual reminder. And, technically, another person shouldn't be memorising someone else's pin number. However, if you do happen to spot a piece of paper bearing a parent's pin number, you could discreetly keep your own file copy, just in case.

Direct debits

These certainly make bill paying simpler. Yet they're not always 'trusted' by older people, especially if they're not long-term bank-account users. If, however, you can persuade parents to start getting monthly bills paid this way – there's often a discount for certain utilities, which is a good incentive – provided you keep a detailed record of the bank details, direct debits, dates and what they're for, this might help ease the problem of regular bill paying.

Becoming a co-signatory

If you have a widowed or divorced parent with fairly simple finances and one cheque account, you could simplify things by becoming a co-signatory to the account, so that your signature can be used as an alternative to theirs, if necessary. Opinion is divided on this, however. Some organisations working on behalf of older people discourage this, saying it puts older people at risk, e.g. an unscrupulous relative could become a co-signatory and clean out the account.

However, if your parent feels comfortable with this idea, both you and they will need to sign forms from the bank confirming you all agree. The bank may also wish to double check all this with your parent by phone and will require proof of your identity.

'He was a terror with money'

Derek is 86 and was widowed six years ago. Until quite recently he lived with his son, Gary, 58, and his daughter-in-law, Donna, 56, in their home just outside Leeds. But Derek's increasing dementia problems became too difficult for the couple to handle because they both work full time. So with great reluctance, they found a nearby care home for Derek where they visit regularly.

'The illness has changed Dad completely, he's very confused and withdrawn now, though he seems to remember us. Before, he was very outgoing, the life and soul of the party – but he was a terror with money, he just couldn't handle it,' explains Gary.

'Mum always had total control of their money – he'd get so much doled out to him a week, though in later years, most of that went in the betting shop. They never bought property or had much saved, which, in the end, meant that the local authority had to stump up for Dad's care-home fees.'

But what the couple didn't realise until Derek moved was that, once widowed, Derek had got into huge debt. First, the couple discovered that Derek had been borrowing money from a loan shark, someone he knew from the local pub. The interest rates were extortionate, several hundred per cent on a few hundred pounds.

'We only found out when the man came round while Derek was out to offer him another loan. We got the truth out of Dad later. He'd actually paid the guy off. But the man wouldn't leave Dad alone. He kept saying Dad was his best customer – and Dad was flattered.'

With considerable effort they persuaded Derek not to borrow again. But not long before he went into the care home, they discovered more debt: Derek had run up a credit-card bill of £4,000, mainly with cash advances.

'We'd never spotted the bills before because he'd collect the post while we were at work. God knows where the money went, probably in the betting shop. He probably paid off the loan shark that way.'

Somehow, Derek had managed to make the minimum monthly repayments at the local bank. Then the dementia started to take hold and he'd stopped. 'As soon as we discovered it, I started paying the minimum repayments,' explains Gary. 'I couldn't see any other way round it.

'But when he went into the care home, I got in touch with the credit-card company again and explained Dad's situation: I was hoping they'd agree to me paying a lower monthly payment.

'When I mentioned Dad's dementia they said if I could get the doctor to confirm in writing that Dad was permanently in a care home with dementia, they'd consider waiving the debt.

'I did what they asked. And they wrote and said they were clos-
ing the account. I was amazed. There was Dad, totally irresponsi-
ble with money to the last, getting completely off the hook.

'You hear so much about banks and credit-card companies
hounding people: you never think about the debt they have to
write off when older people without savings can't honour it any
more.'

Is an enduring power of attorney the best option?

An enduring power of attorney is a legal document in
which a person nominates one or more people (for
instance, their children) to act on their behalf if they lose
the ability to handle their finances.

If your parents are open to the sort of conversation
where this can be discussed, in case they become severely
incapacitated, then you may find this is the easiest way to
resolve the complication of handling all their finances,
especially if there is a family home which may have to be
sold to pay for care-home fees – or if their finances are
complicated.

Whoever is nominated as attorney is legally empowered
as a trusted person to make all financial decisions for their
relative while they are alive. And it entails total management of all their finances, including completing their tax
returns. Without it, a family has no legal authority to make
any financial arrangements for their parents.

New rules regarding power of attorney are now being
introduced for England and Wales. There will be two

different types, both called lasting power of attorney, one covering financial matters and property and the other for decisions about health and welfare issues (allowing a person to appoint someone to speak legally for them on issues of care and medical treatment). In Scotland, you can already nominate a 'welfare attorney', as well as a person to manage financial affairs – called a 'continuing attorney'.

Setting it up

You can either arrange for this to be done through a solicitor, or you can organise it yourself via the Public Guardianship Office (PGO; see Resources, page 259). Both parties have to sign the document. Setting-up costs range from £150 to £300.

Bear in mind, however, that the new rules mean that the power of attorney only becomes legally enforceable once it has been formally registered, a process that can take up to a month. This has been introduced to safeguard against abuse. It cannot, therefore, be used until the registration process is completed and all other family members have been informed. You can register it yourself with the PGO or get a solicitor to do this.

What happens without a power of attorney?

Your parents may, of course, refuse to sign over the responsibility for their finances. Or circumstances might take over before you discuss it; a sudden incapacitating stroke or advanced dementia may mean a person may no longer be able to sign a form, or understand what it means.

In this case, you can apply direct to the Court of Protection (the body responsible for registering enduring power of attorney) and ask to be appointed as your parent's receiver.

You will have to make a very good case and you will be asked to prove your identity. It is more expensive than power of attorney – expect to pay to the court around £500 – and the process itself can take up to six months before the receiver is finally appointed. You may also have to get certain financial transactions checked by the court, particularly if you are selling a family property.

Making a will

Many people never make a will, which creates all sorts of problems after they go, especially if there are considerable assets involved. Making a will means that family and relatives don't have to face a pile of paperwork and financial issues at a time when they may still be struggling with bereavement. But no one can be forced to make a will; you can only suggest they organise one, ideally when they are prepared to sit down and consider all the issues involved.

It costs around £100–£300 to set up a will through a solicitor, depending on area. The more complex and detailed the will, the higher the legal cost.

It is quite likely that in making a will, your parents will appoint you or a sibling as executor. (An executor is a personal representative nominated to administer and distribute their possessions and estate.) Or they may choose a professional executor, a solicitor or accountant, to carry out probate (the term for carrying out the instructions of the will).

Professionals charge fees for their time; this will eventually be deducted from the estate. If parents want to do this, it's an idea to suggest they check fee scales beforehand.

What may encourage your parents to make a will is the fact that a properly written, up-to-date will, organised by a solicitor, is not only the best way of ensuring that all their wishes are carried out after their death – it can be another way of ensuring that the family home is excluded from any means testing for care-home fees (see Chapter 9, Moving, page 168).

Writing a will may also prompt your parents to consider the matter of inheritance tax. With rising house prices in the UK, families are increasingly concerned with seeking ways to minimise the burden for their children when they die. Your parents' solicitor can advise them.

Another point worth remembering and explaining to your parents is that while wills are regarded as a finality, they can always be changed. There are further legal charges to do this. But it is an option which many people overlook.

Families can contest a will. But if a will has been properly drawn up, it may be very difficult to change and it will also involve getting legal advice from a solicitor experienced in disputes, so it may be costly.

Should your parents opt for a DIY will, using a document purchased from most stationers?

This may be an idea if their finances are very simple and straightforward and they just want to leave everything to one or two people. But DIY wills must be witnessed, and if there are any mistakes they may be rendered invalid. Also, less-than-scrupulous relatives have been known to ignore them after the person dies because the contents do not suit their own agendas.

What happens without a will?

Without a will, a person's estate will be distributed by the rules of intestacy – which means that the law decides who gets what. Most married couples believe that if one of them dies without leaving a will, their spouse will inherit everything. This isn't always so. In the case of a married couple with children whose estate is worth less than £250,000, the surviving spouse does receive everything. But if the estate is worth more than £250,000, the surviving spouse receives £250,000 and the right to draw interest from half of anything over £250,000. Their children would then receive half of the sum over £250,000 and be entitled to the remainder on the death of the surviving spouse.

For couples who are not lawfully married but have children, the estate is shared between the children – the intestacy rules do not recognise common-law partners. The term 'children' includes natural, adopted and illegitimate children – but it excludes step-children.

For couples without children, if one dies intestate and leaves an estate worth less than £450,000, then everything goes to the surviving spouse. If the estate is worth more than £450,000, then the surviving spouse receives £450,000 plus half the balance. The remaining balance goes to the other relatives in the following order: parents; brothers/sisters; half-brothers/sisters; grandparents; aunts/uncles; spouses of aunts/uncles.

A relative other than a spouse who is financially dependent on a person who has died without making a will can make an application for provision to the courts, via a solicitor.

For further information, contact your nearest probate office in England and Wales; the Scottish Court Service in Scotland; and the Northern Ireland Court Service in Northern Ireland (see Resources, page 259).

Funeral arrangements

Wills are important too for avoiding family disputes about funeral arrangements because these can be specifically set out in a will. Some people feel very strongly about the way they leave this world – and how they wish to be remembered. They want to choose what sort of funeral they have and even the music they would like played (see Chapter 12, Endings, page 219).

Even if your parents stubbornly refuse to consider any kind of will, it is tremendously helpful to have some kind of conversation with them about their wishes for their funerals. It may be upsetting to ask people you love about this. But if you don't ask, when the time does come – a time when you least need to be unsure – you won't know. And often, elderly people are quite open about their last wishes – it is mainly their relatives who hold back out of fear of upsetting them.

Here are some important questions you might ask your parents about their funeral wishes:

- Would they prefer burial or cremation?
- Do they want the family to view their body after death?
- What kind of service would they prefer: a cemetery or crematorium service, a memorial service, a church service – or no service at all?
- If cremated, what would they want to be done with their ashes?
- Would they like a memorial headstone and is there any wording they would like?
- Would they like a family member to give a eulogy or talk about their life? Are there any particular events or people they would like mentioned?
- What kind of music would they prefer?
- How would they like to be dressed? Would they prefer to wear their wedding ring? Or should it be saved for someone else in the family?
- Do they want flowers? If so, what kind? Would they prefer donations to a particular charity?

Getting advice

If you discover that a parent has run into debt, free confidential advice is available from charities like Citizens Advice, or over the phone by the National Debtline. The

Consumer Credit Counselling Service also offers free professional advice to people with unsecured debt (like credit or store cards).

For free advice on care-home fees, Help the Aged run a care fees advice service. The charity will also provide free factsheets on a range of care-related and legal topics.

Saga also offer a free specialist long-term care-advice service to help parents and families navigate the complex legal and financial issues involved. They also give free advice on wills, enduring powers of attorney and changes in property ownership.

For further information on these charities, see Resources, pages 260–61.

12

Endings

Losing someone close to you is one of life's most dramatic changes – and the most distressing. A parent may have been very old, very ill, or healthy one minute and gone the next, but whichever way it happens, the feeling of loss is bound to be painful and emotionally confusing. You may be shocked, disbelieving, even numb, unable to accept that it has really happened. You might be angry: 'How dare they leave me?' Or, if it's an unexpected death, you may be resentful that fate has robbed you of a chance to say goodbye properly.

Yet when we're facing up to the loss of a parent, even one whose health has been declining for some time, there is no 'right' way or formula when it comes to dealing with all the emotions and confusing feelings loss may bring in its wake.

Coping with loss

Everyone handles loss differently. Some people remain composed and calm, then fall into a heap long after the funeral. Others may cry buckets. Some stay dry-eyed but compelled to create a relentless whirl of activity, organising everything, and keeping so busy they don't have time to face the reality until long after the event.

In the main, you should follow whichever path feels best or most comfortable at the time. This is not the time for behaving in a certain way because you think you 'ought' to. While there are many practical issues to contend with (see page 217), being able to 'go with the flow' emotionally is always better after loss than keeping a tight rein on feelings and leaving them unexpressed.

Losing a parent can be profoundly unsettling because it is such a fundamental, personal loss. One friend told me after losing her father suddenly while they were on holiday: 'The impact isn't just emotional, it's physical too – every single bit of you is affected, like being hit in the chest by a train.' Another took nearly two years to accept losing her mother who had been healthy to the last. 'It wasn't her time to go,' she kept saying. Her mother was 94. My friend just didn't see her mother as being 'old'.

A lot depends too, of course, on the nature of your relationship with the parent who has died. Someone who had a very difficult relationship with a parent may take a long time to get over their loss, perhaps because their feelings of guilt might linger for some time before they can let them go. Conversely, someone in the same family who was much closer might be able to accept it more easily: their emotional responses may be less troubling.

How you cope, of course, will also depend on your belief system. Anyone with strong religious beliefs will find comfort and reassurance in their faith, especially in the difficult months after the loss. But essentially, each one of us looks at the end of life in our own way. So if you can accept death as the only real certainty in life, you'll understand that there's a certain symmetry to losing someone close to you – a cycle, if you like. One part of life comes to an end and those who are left behind go into the next stage of life – without that person.

Understanding your grief

In the first few weeks after someone dies, the need to organise many things may stop you from grieving consciously; you may not really have much time to stop and think.

But once life has gone back to normal, sadness and depression may creep up on you, especially if you've been caring for a parent or spent a lot of time with them in the last weeks or months of their life.

You may feel down, tired and generally unhappy for some time. You may find yourself crying intermittently. Such behaviour is not unusual. It's natural to feel this way. In fact, if the loss of a loved one had very little effect on you, that would be far more worrying. It's also natural to feel angry at the 'unfairness' of it all, of feeling left in the lurch, for instance, or even resentful of others who still have healthy parents. But in most cases, over time, these feelings will diminish and you will start to feel less upset and more accepting of your loss.

However, if your depression becomes serious or anyone else in the family seems to be unable to adjust to life after a bereavement, it may be necessary to contact a GP or seek outside counselling help.

Signs of serious depression include:

- Having no energy at all, even to do the simplest things
- Having little or poor appetite, resulting in weight loss
- Poor sleeping habits (this can mean either sleeping too much or not enough)
- Generally feeling unable to cope with life

It can help a great deal to talk to those closest to you about your feelings and memories of the person who has died. But no one should be ashamed to seek help if depression starts to make serious inroads into their life and health.

Getting help for bereavement

Cruse Bereavement Care offers a free counselling service, advice and information, and local bereavement support groups. The British Association for Counselling and Psychotherapy provides information on specialist counsellors in your area. If I Should Die is a useful website with all kinds of bereavement advice and information on funerals. For further information, see Resources, pages 261–2.

Here are some thoughts to help you cope after the death of a parent:

- Don't imagine that grief will overwhelm you immediately: it may be some time before you actually get to the stage when you can let your emotions out
- You may feel terrible at times but you may also feel inappropriately good sometimes – and worry that this is wrong. It's not. It's perfectly normal.

- Talk about your feelings to family, your partner, close friends or a counsellor. Talking will help a lot.
- Be aware that grief can affect other close relationships and you may feel, fairly or not, that others are not sympathetic enough. Understand that some people find it easier to shut off from others if they're grieving. Try to give them time and space to work it out themselves. But don't stop communicating: this is bound to be a testing time.
- Try writing down how you feel. That gives you a chance to release all sorts of emotions.
- Don't let grief drag you down: you can't afford to neglect your own health, appearance or well-being. Eat regularly and sensibly. Avoid large amounts of alcohol: alcohol is a depressant.
- Try to focus on the fact that you did whatever you could to help – and you did it out of love.
- Understand that the hardest part of grieving is accepting the loss. Once you've accepted that someone is gone, you can start to move forward.

Saying goodbye

If an elderly relative has been ill in hospital for some time, you may, in one sense, have already started to grieve for them before their death because their illness may have 'prepared' the family for the inevitable – and even given everyone a chance to say goodbye.

Having that time to say goodbye is important. It gives people a sense of closure and it's a chance to tell a parent how much you love them – and how good a parent they've been.

Distressing as it may be if your parent is semi-conscious or unable to speak, the words themselves are reassuring for everyone. Perhaps they can't hear you. But later you will probably take great comfort from the fact that you were able to tell them how much you care – when it mattered most of all.

The younger members of the family should, if possible, be encouraged to say goodbye too. Understanding that death is part of life is something that children can deal with quite easily, though adults don't always credit them with this. Even a three- or four-year-old may understand what's happening, if you talk to them carefully about it all beforehand.

Try saying something like: 'Grandma is in bed, she looks very ill, she can hear you – but she might not be able to see you.' And then ask if they want to go and say goodbye to her – 'Because we might not see her again.'

As a parent or grandparent your instinct might be to shield a small child from death and loss. But it's worth noting that hospitals and hospices now actively encourage children to come in to say goodbye to older relatives if time and circumstance permit. This is a far healthier approach to death than the 'hush-it-all-up' scenario we may have known as children.

'We'd all had a chance to tell her we loved her'

Deirdre is 62, a mother of five and grandmother to ten. She has a younger brother, Ken, 58 and a sister, Mo, 60.

Their mother, Brenda, died two years ago at the age of 79. But Deirdre says that because of the somewhat unusual events that took place beforehand, their loss was far less painful than they might have ever imagined.

'Mum started to have heart problems in her sixties,' explains Deirdre. 'She was on medication and regular hospital check-ups for years.'

'One day we got a phone call from her neighbour to say they'd called an ambulance: Mum had complained of serious chest pain and was pale and breathless. By the time we reached the hospital, she'd had a heart attack, a bad one.'

The family kept a vigil at the hospital for two days. Then the doctors said Brenda would pull through. A day later, Deirdre was in her car, sitting in traffic when the hospital rang her. 'They said to get there immediately – Mum was dying.'

Brenda was unconscious but the entire family managed to get there quickly. Each one, in turn, stepped up to hug and kiss her and say their own goodbye.

'We were shocked – but grateful we'd been alerted in time. Then we sat and waited for the end.'

It didn't come. After a couple of hours, Brenda sat up in bed and started chatting quite normally.

'Ooh, it was a lovely place I went to,' she told her children. 'I saw Ian there [Ian was Brenda's late husband who had died many years before] but he pushed me back. I'm not ready to go anywhere yet.'

Amazed by what had happened, the family nonetheless accepted what Brenda was telling them. And they were incredibly relieved to have her back. 'The doctors were obviously shocked when they saw her up and about. They really didn't expect her to live.'

Eighteen months later, the family learned that Brenda had liver cancer. She died within weeks, eventually slipping into a coma. It was a peaceful and very undramatic end.

'It may sound strange but losing Mum like that, in the end, wasn't so bad for any of us because of what had happened. We'd all had a chance to tell her we loved her and say what we wanted to say. In a way, it was as if we'd been given an extra 18 months to get used to the idea of losing her.'

Practical issues

If someone dies at home

Their GP should be contacted immediately. The GP will come to the house to give you a medical certificate of cause of death and information on how to register the death. If the cause of death is unclear, it may be referred to the local coroner's office: the doctor should explain why this is necessary and what to do.

If someone dies in a hospital, hospice or nursing home

You should be able to see them, provided you can get there within a few hours. After that, the hospital or home will usually take the person to their mortuary and you can still see them there, if you choose. The hospital will give you the medical certificate, signed by a doctor, and arrange other details, like a suitable time for you to collect your relative's possessions.

Do remember that hospital or care-home staff may have formed a very close bond with your relative, whom they may have got to know over a period of time. If possible, invite them to the funeral. They'll want to attend if they can.

Registering a death

All deaths have to be registered within five days at a local register office in the area in which the death occurred. (In Scotland you have eight days to register a death.) Check for listings online or in a local phone directory.

Any close relative can register a death, provided they take the medical certificate to the registry office as well as identifying documents like the deceased person's birth and marriage certificates or passport. (The hospital will give you paperwork to explain what you will need to take with you.)

The registrar will give you:

- The death certificate. Always ask for extra copies at the time you register the death; you will need them afterwards for dealing with the will or financial matters. There are nominal charges for these copies.
- The certificate for burial or cremation, to hand to the funeral director once you've chosen one.

Organising the funeral

What helps most of all at this time is knowing your parent's wishes for their funeral, so that their send-off can be organised accordingly (see Chapter 11, Financial issues, page 208).

Your parents may have taken out term life assurance, a life insurance policy that provides a lump-sum payment if someone dies before a certain age, or whole life assurance, which pays out at any age. Or they may have a personal pension scheme from previous employers that pays out a lump sum towards funeral costs. Sometimes parents may have even opted for a prepurchase funeral plan, so that it is already paid for and the details planned, making it easier to organise.

If they've mentioned any of these in the past, it's a good idea to check your parents' paperwork first for details. Some insurers will pay a limited sum on evidence of death, i.e. a death certificate; others will only pay out after probate.

But there are often no arrangements at all. Some people can't or won't confront the details of their own demise. Others may die before they get the chance to do so. This can make organising the funeral itself somewhat more complex. In this case, it's better if the planning is a shared endeavour because there are so many details to consider – though quite often just one person in the family, usually an older sibling or surviving parent, does most of the organising.

Without a parent's last wishes to follow, the funeral planning can be fraught with emotional hurdles: one person might want one thing, the organiser insists on another. The only sensible way to approach this is for everyone to focus on the important question: is this what Mum or Dad would have wanted?

Finding a funeral director

There are around 2,500 professional funeral directors in the
UK. Many people believe you can only contact a funeral
director to discuss arrangements after someone has died.
This isn't the case. A good funeral director is happy to
answer questions and discuss certain issues if someone is
concerned either about their own funeral or that of someone who is ill. Yet again, this is a situation where your own
preplanning can help.

The best way to find a good funeral director is either
through personal recommendation locally or from shopping around. Funerals are big business, worth over £1
billion a year in the UK. As a consequence, while the idea
of shopping for a funeral may seem bizarre, the cost
alone makes it as much of a consumer-led choice as anything else.

These are the things to consider when choosing a funeral
director:

- Check accreditation first. The company should either
  belong to the National Association of Funeral Directors
  (NAFD) or the National Society of Allied and
  Independent Funeral Directors (SAIF; see Resources,
  page 262).
- If possible, obtain quotes from more than one com-
  pany.
- Get a detailed description of costs and a price list when
  getting a quote.
- Ask for telephone quotes to be put in writing.
- A good funeral director is a facilitator who helps the
  family organise as much of the funeral arrangements as

they want. Don't feel obliged to make any decisions before discussing them with the rest of the family.

If you do have any complaints afterwards regarding a funeral director, both the above organisations have independent complaints schemes.

Other funeral options

You can, of course, organise a funeral without a funeral director; there are no legal requirements for what type of funeral ceremony is chosen once a death certificate is registered. This means much closer attention to organising all the details involved but nonetheless, increasing numbers of people choose DIY funerals organised by family as a more personalised farewell – or for some who may wish to be buried in a cardboard coffin, for instance – a greener alternative.

If it is in accordance with your parents' beliefs or wishes, you may opt for a natural burial ground rather than a cemetery or crematorium. There are over 200 of these throughout the UK. For more information, contact the Natural Death Centre, a charity that helps people organise this type of DIY funeral (see Resources, page 262).

If your parents have indicated that they'd prefer a non-religious funeral, you can use a local non-religious celebrant or officiant. Ask the funeral director for details or contact the British Humanist Association for details of officiants in your area (see Resources, page 262).

How much will it cost?

Basic costs for cremation start at around £1,300. Burial costs start from £1,500. Additional optional expenses, like hire cars, flower arrangements, a headstone, a plaque or an upgrade to a more expensive type of coffin, add considerably to the cost. Basic burial costs vary in each area because local authority burial plot fees differ. But a lavish funeral with all the trimmings, including a specially worded headstone, can easily run into several thousand pounds.

Most funeral directors require payment before probate is settled. Bills are usually sent out immediately after the funeral and payment terms are normally within 14 days to one month. If payment is not made after this, interest may be added.

Third-party fees or disbursements usually have to be paid before the funeral. These are smaller charges such as crematorium or organist's fees, or doctor's fees (for the paperwork involved in organising a cremation).

Once you know exactly how much it will all cost, talk to everyone else in the family to work out payment. The simplest way is for one person to pay and be reimbursed after probate. Or you could split the cost between two or three siblings. Normally, a deceased person's bank and building-society accounts are frozen until probate, unless it is a joint account, whereby the co-signatory may be able to pay for the funeral out of these funds (see Chapter 11, Financial issues, page 199). Building societies may be willing to release money prior to probate, but only on production of a death certificate.

In a situation where no one is able to pay for the funeral, the local authority may be able to help. But they will have to be contacted before the funeral takes place.

Anyone receiving Pension Credit, Housing Benefit, Council Tax Benefit or certain other benefits may be eligible for a one-off funeral payment from the Social Fund to help towards funeral expenses. This payment must be paid back from the deceased person's estate and you must claim within three months of the date of the funeral. Contact The Pension Service (see Resources, page 263).

Funeral planning dos and don'ts

- Do make sure you involve everyone who needs to be involved – and invite everyone you think should be there
- Do discuss all details with other close family members: book times, if necessary, for busy siblings
- Don't write or organise a spoken tribute to a parent without making every effort to show it to siblings or a surviving parent (not doing so can create family dissent or bitterness for some time)
- Don't take small children to the funeral without asking them if they want to go – and explaining what will happen
- Don't make any decisions about what happens after cremation without consulting the rest of the family; if there's a surviving partner, the final decision rests with them
- Don't ignore the smaller details of a parent's funeral instructions, even if you don't agree with them. Last wishes really are last wishes

Sharing the loss

Losing a parent affects other close relationships too, especially if one parent survives the other and needs supporting through the painful times after the bereavement.

If anything, this is a tough time when families can bond together and help each other through the worst. Some families do this brilliantly. They may have loved Mum or Dad in different ways. Their individual lives may be quite different. But the loss itself is one they instinctively know how to share.

Other families can be divided by loss: squabbles over the past, financial resentments, and guilt or anger at what wasn't done or said at the time create bitterness and blame. Individual grief may linger or remain unresolved – because it hasn't been shared.

Clearly, sharing your feelings with your family and friends can make a huge difference. And if you're worried about a surviving parent and how they will cope, their loss and feelings may also be quite different from yours. But that shouldn't prevent you and siblings from rallying round to support them.

How do you best support a grieving parent?

You may believe that jollying them out of sadness or trying to perk them up with outings or distractions might help. That might be useful later. But in the weeks after a bereavement, you'd be better off encouraging a parent to express their feelings – the 'go-with-the-flow' approach to releasing emotion that applies for everyone, rather than bottling it up. And if you can share that release together, it will help.

For instance, rather than standing back and saying, 'Oh, you cry, Mum, I'll be here for you,' you'd probably both be better off crying now – and crying together.

If you've already been able to discuss the practical issues about what might happen after one partner goes, then helping a parent through this hard time might be slightly less fraught. For instance, it may have already been decided that another sibling will move to live closer to them. Or you may already know that they are resolute in their decision to remain in their own home and have worked out ways to deal with this.

Avoid having weighty conversations about major issues immediately after someone has died; it isn't always the best time to think through such things. Emotions may be too near the surface. It may be better to give everyone time to come to terms with what's happened. But if you do find yourself having to reorganise a parent's life while simultaneously grieving, consider the following:

- Accept that a surviving parent may suddenly become much more dependent and needy. This is hard if you're struggling with your own grief. So make sure you enlist additional support wherever you can. Then work out what you can do, what others can do, and explain it all to your parents.

- If possible, whatever plans are being made for the future, it's better if the bereaved parent remains in their own home for the first few weeks. Maybe you or another relative can stay with them at first. But if you can't, they may be happy to stay in your home for a while.

- Make time for the things you really enjoy doing: swimming, walking, gym, meditation, perhaps. This isn't selfish or a way of avoiding reality: time spent recovering yourself eventually helps your parent too.

- Don't rush back to work too quickly. Evaluate how you feel.

- When you do go back, find out what support is available at work. Large companies have employment assistance schemes from which you may be able to get some support and counselling.

- If a bereaved parent is obviously struggling emotionally, ask your employer if you can go back on a part-time basis for a set period of time. If you find yourself caring at home full-time for a surviving parent, you now have the right to request flexible working hours (see Chapter 2, Family relationships, page 25).

Keeping the memory alive

When it comes to losing someone you love, particularly if they're very old, many people make the big mistake of setting some sort of time limit on grief. There is a lot of: 'Oh, you've had a year now, time to stop thinking about it.'

You shouldn't set any limit at all. Give yourself as much time as you feel you need to come to terms with your loss. And if you feel counselling will help you, consider waiting a few weeks; research shows that counselling works best once people are no longer in a state of shock.

There are, of course, many emotional hurdles to overcome: birthdays, anniversaries, family celebrations, holidays without your mum or dad. New babies they won't see grow up. Problems or successes you'd normally share with them. Or little things that probably won't matter to anyone else but you.

One woman said her most poignant feelings after her mother's death came months after the funeral – when she changed the curtains. 'Mum and I always did the curtains together, it was something we loved doing,' she told me.

Whichever way it happens to you, what really matters is your gradual adjustment to the fact that they've gone. At the same time, you'll want to keep their memory alive. If that means visiting their grave regularly, talking about them to friends and family or just leafing through photos of happy times occasionally – all these things will aid the process.

Not all relationships with parents follow an easy path, of course. There may have been problems in your relationship; some people even feel a sense of relief that they're no longer around. If you feel a sense of remorse at having such feelings or thoughts, it's better just to accept them, rather than hanging on to them. They're not that uncommon. And whatever type of relationship you had, it doesn't negate the fact that you are now a child without a parent, even if you don't feel a huge sense of loss.

Finally, for those who do feel that loss keenly, it may be very difficult initially. And life will be quite different without them. But by focusing on the good memories of your mum or dad, the fact that they had a good life and, most importantly, shared their love and understanding while they were around, you will eventually notice a gradual shift in your feelings – and an easier acceptance of their passing.

Resources

Throughout the book current sums for benefits and allowances are quoted. Please note that while correct at the time of going to press, these are subject to change. In this section I have supplied contact details for the organisations that control these payments so that you can check for updates.

1 Are there changes ahead?

National Centre for Independent Living
Lists individual local-authority social services departments and contact names.
National Centre for Independent Living, 4th Floor,
Hampton House, 20 Albert Embankment, London SE1 7TJ
Phone: 020 7587 1663
Email: info@ncil.org.uk
www.ncil.org.uk

2 Family relationships

British Association for Counselling and Psychotherapy

The largest professional association of counsellors and psychotherapists in the UK. The BACP advises on standards and ethics, and its website has a useful search facility, to find a qualified therapist.

BACP, BACP House, 15 St John's Business Park, Lutterworth LE17 4HB

Phone: 0870 443 5252

www.bacp.co.uk

Relate – the relationship people

Relate offers advice, relationships counselling, support and consultations, either face to face, on the phone or through their website.

Phone: 0300 100 1234

Email: enquiries@relate.org.uk

www.relate.org.uk

3 Maintaining independence

Care Quality Commission

The CQC inspect and report on care specialists (including private agencies) and councils to improve social care and stamp out bad practice. You can search for a list of care homes and services in your area.

Care Quality Commission, City Gate, Gallowgate, Newcastle on Tyne NE1 4WH

Phone: 03000 61 61 61

Email: enquiries@cqc.org.uk

www.cqc.org.uk

General Social Care Council

The GSCC register social care workers in England, and regulate their conduct and training.

General Social Care Council, Goldings House, 2 Hay's Lane, London SE1 2HB

Phone: 020 7397 5800 (information line: Monday–Friday 10 am–12 pm and 2 pm–4 pm) or 020 7397 5100 (switchboard)

Email: info@gscc.org.uk

www.gscc.org.uk

Age UK

For advice on ageing issues – the UK's largest organisation working with and for older people. Local Age Concern charities offer a wide range of activities and services.

Age UK England, Astral House, 1268 London Road, London SW16 4ER

Freephone advice helpline: 0800 169 6565 (8 am–7 pm every day)

Reception: 020 8765 7200

www.ageuk.org.uk

British Red Cross

Offer excellent short-term support for older people.

British Red Cross, UK Office, 44 Moorfields, London EC2Y 9AL

Phone: 0870 170 7000

Email: information@redcross.org.uk

www.redcross.org.uk

Homeshare International

Homeshare run a scheme for elderly people who are struggling to live alone and need extra help with domestic chores.
Homeshare International, 11 Divinity Road, Oxford
OX4 1LH
Phone: 01865 699990
www.homeshare.org

United Kingdom Homecare Association

For details of private agencies providing assistance with personal care (e.g. washing and dressing) or live-in and nursing care.
UKHCA, Group House, 2nd Floor, 52 Sutton Court Road, Sutton, Surrey SM1 4SL
Phone: 020 8288 5291
Email: helpline@ukhca.co.uk
www.ukhca.co.uk

Homecraft Rolyan

Homecraft Rolyan sell physical-therapy products and equipment solutions to improve the independence and quality of life for those with impaired mobility or a disability.
Homecraft Rolyan, Nunn Brook Road, Huthwaite, Sutton-in-Ashfield, Nottinghamshire NG17 2HU
Phone: 08444 124 330
www.homecraft-rolyan.com

HandyVan Service

Home-support service fitting security equipment to vulnerable people's homes, organised through Help the Aged.
Phone: 01255 473999
www.helptheaged.org.uk

Help the Aged SeniorLink Service
Organises the supply and delivery of security pendant alarms and door-alert buttons. See the website for a downloadable application form.
Phone: 0845 053 2306
www.helptheaged.org.uk

National Neighbourhood Watch Trust
The UK Neighbourhood Watch Trust is a new charitable trust whose primary purpose is to support and promote the neighbourhood watch movement by providing an effective and informative two-way communications channel through its website.
UKNWT, First Floor, 52 London Road, Oadby, Leicester LE2 5DH
Phone: 0116 271 0052
www.neighbourhoodwatch.net

4 Eating and nutrition

Homecraft Rolyan
Homecraft Rolyan sell physical-therapy products and equipment solutions to improve the independence and quality of life for those with impaired mobility or a disability. They stock specially adapted cooking utensils and cutlery.
Homecraft Rolyan, Nunn Brook Road, Huthwaite, Sutton-in-Ashfield, Nottinghamshire NG17 2HU
Phone: 08444 124 330
www.homecraft-rolyan.com

5 Encouraging an active life

RSPCA

Rehomes unwanted or mistreated pets.
Enquiries Service, RSPCA, Wilberforce Way, Southwater,
Horsham, West Sussex RH13 9RS
Phone: 0300 1234 555
www.rspca.org.uk

Blue Cross

Provides animal hospital and adoption services, and pets
for rehoming. Also offers support for pet bereavement.
Blue Cross, Shilton Road, Burford, Oxon OX18 4PF
Phone: 01993 822651
Email: info@bluecross.org.uk
www.bluecross.org.uk

Dogs Trust

The UK's largest dog-welfare charity, offering rehoming,
information and sponsorship.
Dogs Trust, 17 Wakley Street, London EC1V 7RQ
Phone: 020 7837 0006
www.dogstrust.org

Cats Protection

The UK's largest cat-welfare charity specialising in helping,
rehoming and raising awareness.
Cats Protection, National Cat Centre, Chelwood Gate,
Haywards Heath, Sussex RH17 7TT
Phone: 08707 708 649 (switchboard), 08702 099 099
(national helpline) or 08707 708 650 (adoption centre)
Email: helpline@cats.org.uk
www.cats.org.uk

Cinnamon Trust

The national charity for the elderly and their pets. A network of 8,000 volunteers who help owners to care for their pets, e.g. dog walking for housebound owners or fostering pets when owners need hospital care. The Cinnamon Trust's Pet Friendly Care Homes Register lists residential/ nursing homes happy to accept residents with pets. If a pet owner dies they will take on full-time, lifetime care of the pet.

Cinnamon Trust, 10 Market Square, Hayle, Cornwall TR21 4HE

Phone: 01736 757900

Email: admin@cinnamon.org.uk

www.cinnamon.org.uk

Age UK

For advice on ageing issues – the UK's largest organisation working with and for older people. Local Age Concern charities offer a wide range of activities and services.

Age UK England, Astral House, 1268 London Road, London SW16 4ER

Freephone advice helpline: 0800 169 6565 (8 am–7pm every day)

Reception: 020 8765 7200

www.ageuk.org.uk

Contact the Elderly

Local groups organise Sunday afternoon tea parties.

Contact the Elderly, 15 Henrietta Street, London WC2E 8QG

Phone: 0800 716 543

www.contact-the-elderly.org

Volunteering England

For information on how to get involved in volunteering projects in your area.

Volunteering England, Regents Wharf, 8 All Saints Street, London N1 9RL

Phone: 0845 305 6979

Email: volunteering@volunteeringengland.org

www.volunteering.org.uk

Do-it

Over 800,000 opportunities to volunteer all over the UK.

Do-it, 1st Floor, 50 Featherstone Street, London EC1Y 8RT

Phone: 020 7250 5700

www.do-it.org.uk

The Ramblers' Association

Provides information on walking and joining led walks or finding walking companions.

The Ramblers' Association, 2nd Floor, Camelford House, 87–90 Albert Embankment, London SE1 7TW

Phone: 020 7339 8500

Email: ramblers@ramblers.org.uk

www.ramblers.org.uk

Keep Fit Association

Arranges exercise classes enabling people to keep fit together in a relaxed and friendly environment.

Keep Fit Association, 1 Grove House, Foundry Lane, Horsham, West Sussex RH13 5PL

Phone: 01403 266 000

Email: office@emdp.org

www.keepfit.org.uk

Walking the Way to Health Initiative

Find out about walks in your area.

The WHI Team, Natural England, John Dower House, Crescent Place, Cheltenham GL50 3RA

Phone: 0300 060 2287

Email: whiinfo@naturalengland.org.uk

www.whi.org.uk

Tai Chi Union for Great Britain

Provides a list of over 400 registered Tai Chi Chuan instructors throughout Great Britain.

Peter Ballam, Secretary, Tai Chi Union for Great Britain, 5 Corunna Drive, Horsham, West Sussex RH13 5HG (include a stamped, self-addressed envelope)

Email: peterballam@aol.com

www.taichiunion.com

The British Wheel of Yoga

The largest yoga organisation in Britain, with a network of over 3,000 qualified teachers.

BWY Central Office, British Wheel of Yoga, 25 Jermyn Street, Sleaford, Lincolnshire NG34 7RU (send £4.50 for a full information pack)

Phone: 01529 306851

Email: office@bwy.org.uk

www.bwy.org.uk

Natural England

Natural England brings together English Nature, the Countryside Agency and the Rural Development Service. They promote access and recreation in rural and urban

areas, including the Walking the Way to Health Initiative and other health campaigns.
Enquiries, Natural England, Northminster House, Peterborough PE1 1UA
Phone: 0845 600 3078
Email: enquiries@naturalengland.org.uk
www.naturalengland.org.uk

British Healthcare Trades Association

Monitors and maintains standards on products such as wheelchairs, scooters and stairlifts.
British Healthcare Trades Association, New Loom House, Suite 4.06, 101 Back Church Lane, London E1 1LU
Phone: 020 7702 2141
Email: bhta@bhta.net
www.bhta.net

Arthritis Care

Provides advice on living with arthritis.
Arthritis Care, 18 Stephenson Way, London NW1 2HD
Phone: 0845 600 6868 (information line), 0808 800 4050 (confidential helpline) or 020 7380 6500 (switchboard)
Email: info@arthritiscare.org.uk
www.arthritiscare.org.uk

The Walking Stick Shop

Specialises in walking sticks, which are individually tailored to your size. They explain the technique of walking with a cane or stick.
The Walking Stick Shop, 8 & 9 The Old Printing Works, Tarrant Street, Arundel, West Sussex BN18 9JH

Phone: 01903 883796
www.walkingstickshop.co.uk

Driver and Vehicle Licensing Agency

The DVLA can advise on issues surrounding older people and driving. If you are concerned about an elderly relative continuing to drive, you can contact the DVLA by letter or fax with your concerns.

Drivers Medical Group, DVLA, Swansea SA99 1TU
Phone: 0870 600 0301
Fax: 0845 850 0095
www.dvla.gov.uk

6 Getting help

Department for Work and Pensions

Provides benefits and services for pensioners.
Benefit enquiry line: 0800 88 22 00
www.dwp.gov.uk

Department of Health

Supports the NHS and social-care organisations. Offers an information service on social care and the Registered Nursing Care Contribution (RNCC).
Phone: 020 7210 4850
www.dh.gov.uk

The Pension Service

Part of the Department for Work and Pensions, this service will work out the amount of state pension and pension credit that you are entitled to, pay them and answer questions over the phone and by post and email. The Pension Service will also tell you how you can obtain other pension-related entitlements and services.

Phone: 0845 60 60 265 (Monday–Friday 8 am–8 pm)

Winter Fuel Payment helpline: 08459 15 15 15 (Monday–Friday 8.30 am–4.30 pm)

Benefit Enquiry Line: 0800 88 22 00

www.thepensionservice.gov.uk

United Kingdom Homecare Association

The professional association for home-care providers. Use it to find a suitable agency in your area.

UKHCA, Group House, 2nd Floor, 52 Sutton Court Road, Sutton, Surrey SM1 4SL

Phone: 020 8288 5291

Email: helpline@ukhca.co.uk

www.ukhca.co.uk

Care Quality Commission

The CQC inspect and report on care services (including private agencies) and councils to improve social care and stamp out bad practice. You can search for a list of care homes and services in your area.

England:

Care Quality Commission, City Gate, Gallowgate, Newcastle on Tyne NE1 4WH

Phone: 03000 61 61 61

Email: enquiries@cqc.org.uk

www.cqc.org.uk

Scotland:
The Care Commission, Compass House, 11 Riverside
Drive, Dundee DD1 4NY
Phone: 0845 603 0890
www.carecommission.com

Northern Ireland:
Department of Health, Social Services and Public Safety,
Castle Buildings, Stormont, Belfast BT4 3SJ
Phone: 0289 052 0500
Email: webmaster@dhsspsni.gov.uk
www.dhsspsni.gov.uk

Wales:
Care and Social Services Inspectorate Wales, Cathays Park,
Cardiff CF10 3NQ
Phone: 01443 848450
Email: cssiw@wales.gsi.gov.uk
www.csiw.org.uk

Carers UK

The voice of carers. Campaigns on behalf of carers for practical, financial and emotional support.
Carers UK, 20 Great Dover Street, London SE1 4LX
Phone: 0808 808 7777 (Wednesday and Thursday, 10 am–
12 pm and 2 pm–4 pm) or 020 7490 8818
Email: info@carersuk.org
www.carersuk.org

Counsel and Care

Counsel and Care is a charity and advisory service for
people over 60 and their families.

Counsel and Care, Twyman House, 16 Bonny Street,
London NW1 9PG
Phone: 020 7241 8522 or 0845 300 7585 (Monday–
Friday 10 am–12 pm and 2 pm–4 pm, except Wednesday
afternoons)
www.counselandcare.org.uk

The Elderly Accommodation Counsel

A charity whose aim is to help older people make informed
choices about meeting their housing and care needs.
The Elderly Accommodation Counsel, 3rd Floor, 89 Albert
Embankment, London SE1 7TP
Phone: 020 7820 1343
Email: enquiries@eac.org.uk
www.housingcare.org

7 Key health issues

BMJ Best Treatments

Facts about treatment options, based on the latest medical
research.
BMJ Knowledge, BMJ Group, BMA House, Tavistock
Square, London WC1H 9JR
Phone: 020 7383 6995
www.besttreatments.co.uk

Patient UK

Comprehensive, free health information.
www.patient.co.uk

NHS Direct

Information on a range of conditions, surgical procedures, medications and health issues.

Phone: 0845 46 47 (24-hour health advice)

www.nhsdirect.nhs.uk

NHS 24 Scotland

Confidential health advice and information service for people in Scotland.

Phone: 08454 24 24 24 (24-hour health advice)

www.nhs24.com

NHS Direct Wales

Website with a wide range of health information, and an A–Z health encyclopedia.

Phone: 0845 46 47 (24-hour health advice)

www.nhsdirect.wales.nhs.uk

Dr Foster

Website with useful data on doctors, consultants and hospitals across the UK.

www.drfoster.co.uk/public.asp

Age UK

Information and advice on health issues for elderly people.

Age UK England, Astral House, 1268 London Road, London SW16 4ER

Freephone advice helpline: 0800 169 6565 (8 am–7 pm, every day)

Reception: 020 8765 7200

To find your local branch and their nail-cutting service go to their website:
www.ageuk.org.uk

Podiatry Pages
Website with information on podiatry clinics around the UK.
www.podiatrypages.co.uk

The Sleep Council
Advice and tips on how to improve sleep quality and the importance of getting a good night's sleep.
The Sleep Council, High Corn Mill, Chapel Hill, Skipton, North Yorkshire BD23 1NL
Phone: 0845 058 4595
Insomnia Helpline: 020 8994 9874 (Monday–Friday 6pm–8 pm)
To order an information leaflet, phone: 0800 018 7923
www.sleepcouncil.com

Prescription Pricing Authority (PPA) Patient Services
Information on NHS prescription and treatment costs and payment options.
Phone: 0845 850 1166 (England, Scotland and Wales only)

NHS Dentists
For information on finding an NHS dentist, visit:
www.nhs.uk

British Dental Association
Provides a list of about 6,000 dentists in the UK.
www.bda-findadentist.org.uk

Royal National Institute of the Blind

Information, support and advice for people with sight problems.

Royal National Institute of the Blind, 105 Judd Street, London WC1H 9NE

Phone: 0845 766 9999

www.rnib.org.uk

Royal National Institute for Deaf People

Information and support for deaf and hard of hearing people.

Royal National Institute for Deaf People,
19–23 Featherstone Street, London EC1Y 8SL

Phone: 0808 808 0123

Textphone: 0808 808 9000

Email: informationline@rnid.org.uk

www.rnid.org.uk

Adviceguide

The Citizens Advice Bureau online resource is a useful contact for factsheets on health-related costs.

www.adviceguide.org.uk

Arthritis Care

Information and support for people with arthritis.

Arthritis Care, 18 Stephenson Way, London NW1 2HD

Phone: 0808 800 4050 (confidential helpline) or
020 7380 6500 (switchboard)

Email: info@arthritiscare.org.uk

www.arthritiscare.org.uk

Alzheimer's Society

The UK's leading care and research charity for people with dementia, their families and carers.

Alzheimer's Society, Gordon House, 10 Greencoat Place, London SW1P 1PH

Phone: 0845 300 0336

www.alzheimers.org.uk

Carers UK

Provides support and advice for carers and families of people with Alzheimer's.

Carers UK, 20 Great Dover Street, London SE1 4LX

Phone: 0808 808 7777 (Wednesday and Thursday, 10 am–12 pm and 2 pm–4 pm) or 020 7490 8818

Email: info@carersuk.org

www.carersuk.org

Macmillan Cancer Support

For information, practical advice and support for cancer patients, their families and carers.

Macmillan Cancer Support, 89 Albert Embankment, London SE1 7UQ

Free Helpline: 0808 800 1234 (Monday–Friday 9 am–8 pm)

Switchboard: 020 7840 7840 (Monday–Friday 9 am–5.30 pm)

Info: 0800 500 800

www.macmillan.org.uk

for dementia

for dementia run a specialist helpline with advice from Admiral Nurses, specialists in all aspects of dementia care.

for dementia, 6 Camden High Street, London NW1 0JH

Phone: 0845 257 9406 (Admiral Nurses direct) or

020 7874 7210 (switchboard)

www.fordementia.org.uk

MIND

Working to create a better life for everyone with experience
of mental health problems.

MIND, 15–19 Broadway, London E15 4BQ

Phone: 0845 766 0163 (helpline) or 020 8519 2122
(switchboard)

Email: contact@mind.org.uk

www.mind.org.uk

British Association for Counselling and Psychotherapy

The largest professional association of counsellors and psychotherapists in the UK. The BACP advises on standards
and ethics, and its website has a useful search facility, to
find a qualified therapist.

BACP, BACP House, 15 St John's Business Park, Lutterworth
LE17 4HB

Phone: 0870 443 5252

www.bacp.co.uk

Depression Alliance

The UK's leading charity for people affected by depression –
providing information and support services.

Depression Alliance, 212 Spitfire Studios, 63–71 Collier
Street, London N1 9BE

Phone: 0845 123 23 20 (to request an information pack)

Email: information@depressionalliance.org

www.depressionalliance.org

Diabetes UK
The largest organisation in the UK working for people with diabetes, funding research, campaigning and helping people who live with the condition.
Diabetes UK, Macleod House, 10 Parkway, London NW1 7AA
Phone: 020 7424 1000
Email: info@diabetes.org.uk
www.diabetes.org.uk

British Heart Foundation
Information on heart conditions and advice on how to keep your heart healthy.
British Heart Foundation, 14 Fitzhardinge Street, London W1H 6DH
Information line: 0845 070 8070
Switchboard: 020 7935 0185
www.bhf.org.uk

Tena
Products for bladder weakness and incontinence.
Advice line: 0845 30 80 80 30
www.tena.co.uk

The Bladder and Bowel Foundation
Information and support for people with bladder and bowel problems.
The Bladder and Bowel Foundation, Satra Innovation Park, Rockingham Road, Kettering, Northants NN16 9JH
Switchboard: 020 8329 6200

Email: info@bladderandbowelfoundation.org
www.bladderandbowelfoundation.org.uk

National Osteoporosis Society

Information and support for people with osteoporosis.
National Osteoporosis Society, Camerton, Bath BA2 0PJ
Helpline: 0845 450 0230 (Monday–Friday 10 am–3 pm)
Information line: 0845 130 3076 (Monday–Friday 10 am–
4 pm)
Email: nurses@nos.org.uk or info@nos.org.uk
www.nos.org.uk

Cancer Research UK

Provides information about cancer and supports research
into cancer treatment in the UK.
Cancer Research UK, BO Box 123, Lincoln's Inn Fields,
London WC2A 3PX
Phone: 0800 226 237 (to contact a cancer information
nurse) or 020 7242 0200
www.cancerresearchuk.org
www.cancerhelp.org.uk

Stroke Association

Information and support for people affected by stroke.
Stroke Information Service, Stroke House, 240 City Road,
London EC1V 2PR
Helpline: 0845 3033 100 (Monday–Friday 9 am–5 pm)
www.stroke.org.uk

NHS Direct

Information on a wide range of health issues.

Phone: 0845 46 47 (24-hour health advice)

www.nhsdirect.nhs.uk

www.nhs24.com (Scotland)

www.nhsdirect.wales.nhs.uk (Wales)

8 Hospital

Private Healthcare UK

Over 2,500 UK private consultants listed plus all UK private hospitals.

www.privatehealth.co.uk

BUPA

Provides private healthcare insurance, hospitals and health-care services.

Information line: 0800 600 500

Self-pay treatment enquiry line: 0800 434 6600 (for information about one-off BUPA treatment costs for those without private health insurance)

www.bupa.co.uk

BMI Healthcare

Provide 49 acute-care private patient hospitals around the UK.

BMI Healthcare, 66 Chiltern Street, London W1U 6GH

Phone: 020 7009 4500

Email: info@bmihealthcare.co.uk

www.bmihealthcare.co.uk

Nuffield Health

A not-for-profit group of independent hospitals.
Nuffield House, 40–44 Coombe Road, New Malden, Surrey
KT3 4QF
Switchboard: 020 8329 6200
www.nuffieldhealth.org.uk

Community Health Councils (Wales)

Working to enhance and improve the quality of health
services in Wales.
Phone: 0845 644 7814 (to find your local community
health council)
www.wales.nhs.uk

Patient and Client Council (Northern Ireland)

Working to improve health and social-services provision in
Northern Ireland.
Phone: 0800 917 0222 or 028 90 321230
www.patientclientcouncil.hscni.net

Care Quality Commission

Health watchdog in England, ensuring quality of care for
all.
Care Quality Commission, City Gate, Gallowgate,
Newcastle on Tyne NE1 4WH
Phone: 03000 61 61 61
Email: enquiries@cqc.org.uk
www.cqc.org.uk

The Welsh Assembly

For complaints about NHS or private treatment in Wales.
Phone: 0845 010 3300
www.wales.gov.uk

The Care Commission of Scottish Social Services Council

For complaints about care services in Scotland. The Care Commission regulates over 15,000 independent healthcare services in Scotland.
The Scottish Care Commission, Compass House,
11 Riverside Drive, Dundee DD1 4NY
Phone: 0845 603 0890 or 01382 207100
www.carecommission.com

The Healthcare Ombudsman

For complaints about the NHS in England.
The Parliamentary and Health Service Ombudsman,
Millbank Tower, Millbank, London SW1P 4QP
Helpline: 0345 015 4033 (Monday–Friday 8 am–6 pm)
Email: phso.enquiries@ombudsman.org.uk
www.ombudsman.org.uk

The Patients Association

A useful source of help and information for patients.
The Patients Association, PO Box 935, Harrow, Middlesex HA1 3YJ
Helpline: 0845 608 44 55
Email: mailbox@patients-association.com
www.patients-association.org.uk

British Red Cross
Offer excellent short-term support for older people. They provide volunteer workers who visit the home, assisting with simple domestic tasks, usually after a hospital stay or following an accident.
British Red Cross, UK Office, 44 Moorfields, London EC2Y 9AL
Phone: 0870 170 7000
Email: information@redcross.org.uk
www.redcross.org.uk

9 Moving

ERoSH (Sheltered Housing)
Promotes best practice among housing professionals working with older people. The organisation works for better housing choices, and works with the Elderly Accommodation Counsel to provide information on housing and care.
ERoSH, PO Box 2616, Chippenham, Wiltshire SN15 1WZ
Phone: 01249 654249
Email: info@shelteredhousing.org
www.shelteredhousing.org

The Elderly Accommodation Counsel
Information and advice on housing and care issues, for elderly people and their carers.
EAC, 3rd Floor, 89 Albert Embankment, London SE1 7TP
Phone: 020 7820 1343
Email: enquiries@eac.org.uk
www.housingcare.org

The Hanover Housing Association

A leading provider of extra-care schemes in England.
The Hanover Housing Association, Hanover House,
1 Bridge Close, Staines TW18 4TB
Phone: 01784 446000
www.hanover.org.uk

Anchor Trust

Provides good quality sheltered and extra-care housing to
rent or buy.
Anchor Retirement Housing, Milestone Place, 100 Bolton
Road, Bradford BD1 4DH
Phone: 01274 381600
www.anchor.org.uk

MHA Care Group (Methodist Homes for the Aged)

Provides good quality sheltered and extra-care housing to
rent or buy.
MHA Care Group, Epworth House, Stuart Street, Derby
DE1 2EQ
Phone: 01332 296200
Email: enquiries@mha.org.uk
www.methodisthomes.org.uk

BUPA Care Homes

Provides residential and nursing homes to cater for a range
of needs.
BUPA Care Services, Bridge House, Outwood Lane,
Horsforth, Leeds LS18 4UP
Phone: 0800 00 10 10
www.bupacarehomes.co.uk

Retirement villages

Hartrigg Oaks, York, run by the Joseph Rowntree Housing Trust
www.jrf.org.uk
Westbury Fields, Bristol, run by the St. Monica Trust
www.ourservices.stmonicatrust.org
Ryfields, Warrington, near Liverpool, run by Arena Housing
www.housingcare.org.uk
Denham Garden Village, Buckinghamshire, run by the Anchor Trust
www.anchor.org.uk

Counsel and Care

Counsel and Care is a charity and advisory service for people over 60 and their families.
Counsel and Care, Twyman House, 16 Bonny Street, London NW1 9PG
Phone: 020 7241 8522 or 0845 300 7585 (Monday–Friday 10 am–12 pm and 2 pm–4 pm, except Wednesday afternoons)
www.counselandcare.org.uk

Saga

Offer a free specialist long-term care advice service.
Phone: 0800 056 6101 (care advice)
www.saga.co.uk

Help the Aged

Offer a care fees advice service and information on all aspects of financial planning for elderly people.

Help the Aged Care Fees Advice, FREEPOST LON18542,
Oxford OX29 4BR
Phone: 0500 76 74 76 (Monday–Friday 9 am–5 pm)
www.ageuk.org.uk

Care Quality Commission

Their website provides the latest inspection report of each
care home in England.
Phone: 03000 61 61 61
Email: enquiries@cqc.org.uk
www.cqc.org.uk
For homes in Wales: www.csiw.org.uk.
In Scotland: www.carecommission.com

The Registered Nursing Home Association

Provides national information on nursing homes, with lists
of homes in each area.
RNHA, John Hewitt House, Tunnel Lane, Off Lifford Lane,
Kings Norton, Birmingham B30 3JN
Phone: 0800 074 0194 or 0121 451 1088
Email: info@rhna.co.uk
www.rnha.co.uk

HousingCare.org

This website, run by the Elderly Accommodation Counsel,
provides lists of all UK care homes as well as advice and
information on every aspect of moving home.
EAC, 3rd Floor, 89 Albert Embankment, London SE1 7TP
Phone: 020 7820 1343
Email: enquiries@eac.org.uk
www.housingcare.org

Care Quality Commission
For care-home complaints in the UK.
Phone: 03000 61 61 61

The Care and Social Services Inspectorate Wales
Phone: 01443 848450

The Offices of the Care Commission (Scotland)
Phone: 0845 603 0890

Lions Clubs
For the Message in a Bottle scheme.
Lions Clubs International, Multiple District 105 (Great
Britain and Ireland), 257 Alcester Road South, Kings
Heath, Birmingham B14 6DT
Phone: 0845 833 9502
Email: mdhq@lions.org.uk
www.lionsmd.105.org

MedicAlert
This is also run by Lions Clubs. A bracelet or necklet details
the wearer's essential emergency information.
MedicAlert, 1 Bridge Wharf, 156 Caledonian Road,
London N1 9UU
Phone: 0800 581 420
Email: info@medicalert.org.uk
www.medicalert.org.uk

10 What about me?

Carers UK
Their website provides details of local branches offering carers support and information across the UK.
Carers UK, 20 Great Dover Street, London SE1 4LX
Phone: 0808 808 7777(Wednesday and Thursday, 10 am–12 pm and 2 pm–4 pm) or 020 7490 8818
Email: info@carersuk.org
www.carersuk.org

Carer's Allowance Unit
Information about claiming Carer's Allowance.
Phone: 01253 856 123
www.direct.gov.uk/en/CaringForSomeone/index.htm

The Princess Royal Trust for Carers
Offers advice as well as support groups for carers and useful discussion boards.
England: Unit 14, Bourne Court, Southend Road, Woodford Green, Essex 1G8 8HD
Phone: 0844 800 4361
Email: help@carers.org

Scotland: Charles Oakley House, 125 West Regent Street, Glasgow G2 2SD
Phone: 0141 221 5066
Email: infoscotland@carers.org

Wales: 250 Cowbridge Road, East Cardiff CF5 1GZ
Phone: 02920 221788
Email: aedmunds@carers.org
www.carers.org

Crossroads Care

Crossroads have schemes in England and Wales to provide practical support for carers, to allow them time to themselves.

Crossroads Association, 10 Regent Place, Rugby, Warwickshire CV21 2PN

Phone: 0845 450 0350

www.crossroads.org.uk

11 Financial issues

Public Guardianship Office

Responsible for ensuring that receivers or attorneys are appointed to look after the financial affairs of those who are not mentally capable of doing it themselves.

Public Guardianship Office, Archway Tower, 2 Junction Road, London N19 5SZ

Enduring power of attorney helpline: 0845 330 2963 (Monday–Friday 9 am–5 pm)

Phone: 0845 330 2900

Email: customerservice@publicguardian.gsi.gov.uk

www.publicguardian.gov.uk

Probate offices in England and Wales

Probate helpline: 0845 30 20 900

www.hmrc.gov.uk

Sheriff Courts Service

Phone: 0131 229 9200

www.scotcourts.gov.uk

Probate & Matrimonial Courts in Northern Ireland
Phone: 028 9032 8594
www.courtsni.gov.uk

Citizens Advice Bureau
Advice and information on legal, financial and other problems. Visit the website to find your local branch.
www.citizensadvice.org.uk

National Debtline
For confidential, free advice on debt.
National Debtline, Tricorn House, 51–53 Hagley Road,
Edgbaston, Birmingham B16 8TP
Phone: 0808 808 4000 (Monday–Friday 9 am–9 pm,
Saturday 9.30 am–1 pm)
www.nationaldebtline.co.uk

Consumer Credit Counselling Service
Offers free professional advice to people with unsecured debt.
Consumer Credit Counselling Service, Wade House,
Merrion Centre, Leeds LS2 8NG
Phone: 0800 138 1111 (Monday–Friday 8 am–8 pm)
Email: contactus@cccs.co.uk
www.cccs.co.uk

Help the Aged
Offer a care fees advice service and information on all aspects of financial planning for elderly people.
Help the Aged Care Fees Advice, FREEPOST LON18542,
Oxford OX29 4BR

Phone: 0500 76 74 76 (Monday–Friday 9 am–5 pm)
www.ageuk.org.uk

Senior Line for Age UK

Senior Line is an advice line providing information for older people with problems, e.g. with benefits and pensions.
Phone: 0800 169 6565 or 0808 808 7575 (Age Northern Ireland); 029 2043 1555 (Wales Age Cymru); 0845 125 9732 (Age Scotland)
www.ageuk.org.uk

Saga

Offer a free specialist long-term care-advice service. Also give free advice on long term care annuities.
Phone: 0800 056 6101 (care advice) or 0800 556 7997 (long term care annuities)
www.saga.co.uk

12 Endings

Cruse Bereavement Care

Offers a free counselling service, advice and information, and local bereavement support groups.
Cruse Bereavement Care, PO Box 800, Richmond, Surrey TW9 1RG
Phone: 0844 477 9400 (helpline)
Email: helpline@cruse.org.uk (helpline) or info@cruse.org.uk (general email)
www.cruse.org.uk

British Association for Counselling and Psychotherapy

The largest professional association of counsellors and psychotherapists in the UK. The BACP advises on standards and ethics, and its website has a useful search facility, to find a qualified therapist.

BACP, BACP House, 15 St John's Business Park, Lutterworth LE17 4HB

Phone: 0870 443 5252

www.bacp.co.uk

If I Should Die

A useful website with all kinds of bereavement advice and information on funerals.

www.ifishoulddie.co.uk

National Association of Funeral Directors (NAFD)

Support and information on organising funerals in the UK.

618 Warwick Road, Solihull, West Midlands B91 1AA

Phone: 0845 230 1343

Email: info@nafd.org.uk

www.nafd.org.uk

National Society of Allied and Independent Funeral Directors (SAIF)

Information on independent funeral directors in the UK.

SAIF Business Centre, 3 Bullfields, Sawbridgeworth, Hertfordshire CM21 9DB

Phone: 0845 230 6777

www.saif.org.uk

The Natural Death Centre

A charity that helps people organise environmentally friendly and DIY funerals.

The Natural Death Centre, The Hill House, Watley Lane, Twyford, Winchester SO21 1QX

Phone: 0871 288 2098

Email: contact@naturaldeath.org.uk

www.naturaldeath.org.uk

British Humanist Association

Provides details of non-religious officiants in your area.

British Humanist Association, 1 Gower Street, London WC1E 6HD

Phone: 020 7079 3580

Email: info@humanism.org.uk

www.humanism.org.uk

The Pension Service

The Pension Service will tell you whether you are eligible for a one-off funeral payment to contribute towards funeral expenses.

Phone: 0845 60 60 265 (Monday–Friday 8 am–8 pm)

(0845 60 60 275 in Wales)

www.thepensionservice.gov.uk

Index